STONES OF HOPE

ESSAYS, SERMONS AND PRAYERS ON RELIGION AND RACE

VOLUME 3

Sis. Wilhelmina Young.
Grace + Peace to you —
Blessings —
Pastor C. Anthony Hunt
5/6/10

Stones Of Hope
Essays, Sermons, and Prayers on Religion and Race
Volume 3
by C. Anthony Hunt

The Rhodes-Fulbright Library series

ISBN: 978-1-55605-468-6

Ebook: 978-1-55605-469-3

Library of Congress Control Number: 2017959465

Cover Design by: Kristen E. Hunt

WYNDHAM HALL PRESS

www.wyndhamhallpress.com

Printed in The United States of America

ACKNOWLEDGEMENTS

For me, this volume is essentially a testament of hope – hope in God and hope for humanity. And it is out of this hope that I believe that dreams, visions and possibilities for a better world are born. Mine is a hope for a brighter future, a hope that love would abound among all of God's people – a bright hope for tomorrow.

I believe that hope is the window that God has given us to see into God's preferred future for our lives. In the midst of the apparent hopelessness, nothingness, meaninglessness and lovelessness that seem to pervade our collective reality today, hope lends credence to the promises and possibilities that God has for each of our lives. So we are encouraged – regardless of the circumstances that confront us - to keep hoping, for indeed we know that with hope - our best days and our most blessed days are not behind us, but ahead of us.

Emily Dickenson intimated in a poem:

"Hope" is the thing with feathers--
That perches in the soul,
And sings the tune without the words,
And never stops - at all—

I am grateful to God for my family – Lisa, my wife, and the three young adults we have parented, Marcus (deceased), Kristen and Brian. In each of their lives, I see the embodiment of hope. And for my father, William Delaney Hunt, I am always thankful. I dedicate this volume to my now deceased mother, Amelia Mae Hunt who taught me to always speak truth, seek peace with justice, and to abide in hope.

To Epworth Chapel United Methodist Church in Baltimore, Maryland – the church where I serve as pastor, I express my gratitude for what you have taught me about hope through the faith that we live and breathe on a daily basis. I am also grateful for the places where I am privileged to teach – the Ecumenical Institute Theology, St. Mary's Seminary and University in Baltimore, MD, Wesley Theological Seminary in Washington, DC, the Graduate Theological Foundation in Mishawaka, Indiana, and United Theological Seminary in Dayton, Ohio. The students, administration and faculty colleagues in each of these academic settings have taught me much about hope – and have allowed me to flesh out the construct in ways that I pray bring fresh insight and perspective to the church and the world today. Together, we bear witness to the hope that must abound for the world to become a better place.

Recently, I have had a chance to re-read Dr. Jürgen Moltmann's book, *Theology of Hope.* Moltmann shares that "Hope alone is to be called 'realistic', because it alone takes seriously the possibilities with which all reality is fraught. It does not take things as they happen to stand or to lie, but as progressing, moving things with possibilities of change. Only as long as the world and the people in it are in a fragmented and experimental state which is not yet resolved, is there any sense in earthly hopes." (1993, 25)

Finally, Rev. Dr. Martin Luther King, Jr. intimated in his famous "I Have a Dream" speech in 1963 that his prayer was that "there would be hewn out of the mountain of despair, a stone of hope." May Dr. King's dream become a reality in the days that are ahead of us.

-1-

A THANKSGIVING PRAYER

FOR THE NATION AND THE WORLD (2016)

God of our weary years, God of our silent tears; thou who has brought us thus far along the way. Thou who has by thy might, led us into the light – keep us forever in thy path we pray.

(James Weldon Johnson)

O God, you see all and know all – and amidst the various and sundry vicissitudes of life, we are mindful that you are in control of all that is and is to be. We pause to offer thanks to you for your grace and mercy towards us. We are a people of divergent perspectives, with a diversity of hopes, dreams and visions. But we come before you acknowledging the commonality that all persons share in you, the creator of the universe.

O God, we offer you thanks for this nation. We take this opportunity to offer prayers for the nation and our world. We pray for the people of every city and county in every state in America. We pray that you would bless every home and every community – every school and every place where your people gather for work and leisure. Bless those persons who are older and those who are younger. We pray for peace and safety for all of us who live and move throughout every community across our nation, and we pray likewise for communities like ours around the world.

Lord God, we pray especially for your blessings upon those persons who bear the burdens of want and disparity among us – whether it is for lack of food or shelter, inadequate healthcare or inadequate education.

We ask your blessings upon those who serve and lead the nation in elective and appointive office, and those who will do so in the future. Bless them with a portion of your wisdom, patience, integrity, justice and compassion.

"Now drop thy still dews of quietness; let all of our strivings cease; take now from our souls the strain and the stress; and let our ordered lives confess; the beauty of your peace."

(Howard Thurman)

Again, it is with grateful hearts that we pray. Amen.

-2-

STONES OF HOPE REFLECTIONS ON THE MARCH ON WASHINGTON (1963-2013)

(This essay was published in the United Methodist Connection of the Baltimore-Washington Conference of the United Methodist Church in August 2013 on the occasion of the 50th Anniversary observance of the March on Washington (August 28, 1963).)

In just a few days on August 28, 2013, thousands of people from around the nation and world will gather in Washington, DC for the 50th year anniversary and commemoration of the historic March on Washington. Deemed in 1963 as the March for Jobs and Freedom, the march came at the height of the American Civil Rights movement, as over 200,000 persons gathered to call the nation to action as it regarded the rights of all people to economic opportunity, equality and justice.

Among those who spoke at the Lincoln Memorial on that sunlit day in 1963 was the Rev. Dr. Martin Luther King, Jr. King shared with the crowd, the nation and the world a compelling dream – a vision of *Beloved Community* and a world where every "child would be judged not by the color of their skin, but by the content of their character." He articulated a hope that America would live up to the true meaning of its creed as found in the Declaration of

Independence, "We hold these truths to be self-evident, that all (people) are created equal."

For the masses that will gather this year in Washington, DC, this will be a time of remembering, honoring, celebrating, and hopefully renewing a commitment to King's (and others') dream of peace, justice and equality among us.

One of the things that King intimated in his 1963 speech was a hope that God would "hew out of the mountain of despair, a stone of hope." The despair that he was alluding to then was capsulated in what he deemed to be the "triplets of evil" – racism, poverty (classism) and war (militarism). In King's estimation, these were the major categories of the social dis-ease that afflicted America then, and thus there was the need for the struggle for civil rights, human rights and equal rights, and a need for the March on Washington and a renewed call/commitment to action.

For King, Christian hope served as the foundation for his vision of *Beloved Community.* In one of his later sermons, "The Meaning of Hope," he defined hope as that quality which is "necessary for life.' King asserted that hope was to be viewed as "animated and undergirded by faith and love." In his mind, if you had hope, you had faith in something. Thus, for him, hope shares the belief that "all reality hinges on moral foundations." It was, for King, the refusal to give up "despite overwhelming odds." (Baker-Fletcher, 1993, 132)

Today, many people would agree that a great deal of progress has been made in light of King's dream and the call to action in 1963. With the passage of the Civil Rights Act and Voting Rights Act in 1964 and 1965 respectively, greater opportunities for many women and persons of color in our society, the election in 2008 of the first American president of African descent, and expanding engagement of persons across cultures and classes in many cases, we have seen signs of the realization of King's dream.

Yet, as thousands will gather in Washington, DC this week, there is much that continues to ail our nation and the world – including persistent and widespread poverty, inequality and a shrinking middle class, ongoing wars and global conflict with seemingly little or no justification for them and no end in sight, ongoing street violence and gun violence, an American prison industrial complex that continues to expand resulting in the over-incarceration of Black and Brown people, the lack of affordable and adequate healthcare for millions, and disparities in educational achievement across race and class lines. Thus, there's the need to renew our commitment to King's dream, and to heed a call to action.

Every few years, I have the privilege of teaching a group of scholars from Wesley Theological Seminary in a doctoral course that retraces many of the steps of the Civil Rights movement in Alabama. The group that journeyed together to Alabama last summer (2012) was very typical of others over the years. We reflected much of the diversity of society today. We were Hispanic, Native American, white and black, female and male, Baptist, Episcopalian, African Methodist Episcopal and United Methodist. We prayed, sang and shared our thoughts together. As we traveled, my memory harkened back to one of our earlier trips, where Dr.

Eileen Guenther, a professor at Wesley Seminary who was a part of an earlier study group in Alabama, offered that it was a spiritual sung by many choirs, "I'm Gonna Sit at the Welcome Table," that played in her head throughout our experience (see *The American Organist*, November 2008). Dr. Guenther said that she thought about the variety of tables that we encountered as we traveled through Alabama:

- Lunch counters of restaurants where all had not been welcome (in the past);
- The dining room table in the parsonage of Dexter Avenue Baptist Church, in Montgomery, where we were told, the Southern Christian Leadership Conference was formed;
- The kitchen table of the same parsonage where Dr. King searched his soul and felt God telling him to press on with his work;
- The tables at which the people at 16th Street Baptist Church served us lunch, tables placed adjacent to the site of the tragic bombing on September 15, 1963 that killed four young girls;
- The tables around which members of our group gathered to share stories as victims of discrimination, of their courageous work in the Civil Rights movement (and other freedom movements), and their lament over a lack of awareness of what was going on at that time in our country's history.

For me, these are some of the stones of hope hewn out of the mountains of despair among us that King spoke about in August 1963.

And so, each year, we journey with the confirmation class from Epworth Chapel UMC, the church where I serve as pastor, to the site of the Martin Luther King, Jr. Memorial in Washington, DC. Although our group is always much smaller than the one that will gather in a few days in D.C., I sense that our young people and all who journey to the King Memorial day-by-day, glean a sense of what King meant when he dreamt of such stones of hope.

This hope beckons us to love everybody – both our enemies and allies. This hope helps us to see that we can resist giving up on one another because our lives together are animated by the belief that God is present in each and every one of us. It is a hope that all of us might realize and live, and one that can move us ever closer toward becoming *Beloved Community*.

-3-

HOLDING ONTO HOPE

(This address was delivered to the Jefferson County NAACP, First Baptist Church, Chillicothe, OH in January 16, 2011 at the Annual Dr. Martin Luther King, Jr. Celebration.)

On the occasion of the 82nd anniversary of the birth of the Rev. Dr. Martin Luther King, Jr. and almost two years after the historic inauguration of Barack Obama as the 44th president of the United States, we continue to experience unprecedented change and challenge across virtually every sector of our society. From the collapse of the U.S. economy that has affected all of us – to the wars that are now being fought in at least two places in the Middle East – to the proliferation of violence that affects many of our communities - to the healthcare crisis that results in millions of Americans continuing to live without affordable and adequate healthcare today, these are days of unprecedented change and challenge.

For many people across the nation and world, Barack Obama's historic election as the first president of African descent renewed (or birthed) a sense of hope. His election seemed to point - for many - to glimmers of hope that our society had somehow arrived at our ideals of *"e pluribus unum"* (out of many one), and the creed shared in our nation's Declaration of Independence, "We hold these truths to be self-evident, that all (persons) are created equal."

Many people also seemed to sense (and hope) that the election of Obama had ushered in an age of post-racialism and post-racism in America – and perhaps across the world. Two years later, we discover that we as a nation are continuing to come to grips with the racial and racist realities that continue to afflict us.

In the period since Obama's election in November 2008, numerous events have served to heighten our awareness as to the ongoing problems of race and racism in America. Among these events are the contentious Supreme Court confirmation hearings of Justice Sonia Sotomayor (the first Hispanic person to be nominated and confirmed to the nation's highest court); the arrest of distinguished Harvard University Professor Henry Louis Gates at his home in Cambridge, MA; debate surrounding the president's September 2009 speech to students returning to schools across the nation; and the heckling by U.S. Congressman Joe Wilson (South Carolina) during a speech by President Obama to a joint session of the U.S. Congress earlier in 2009.

We recall that in the days leading up to the vote on healthcare reform last March (2010), there seemed to be a heightened air of racial tension and hatred with the new prominence of the Tea Party and other factions who seem intent on "taking back their country." One African-

American congressman, Emanuel Cleaver, (Missouri, who also happens to be a United Methodist minister) was spat upon, apparently by someone opposing healthcare reform. The passage and enactment of the Affordable Care Act (also known as Obamacare), which offers the real possibility that more than 32 million more American citizens will have full access to healthcare, was followed in April by the Governor of Arizona, Jan Brewer, signing into law legislation which serves to target and profile immigrants in that state, and which seems to threaten the freedom of many law abiding persons. In the days following the passage of the Arizona legislation, I received word that one of my nieces – born, raised and educated in a multiracial American family, an honor graduate of a major American research university, and traveling "legally" to Guatemala for her job - upon returning to the U.S. - was detained for a very long period of time in an Arizona airport – apparently because she looked like an "immigrant."

During a recent visit to the Southern Poverty Law Center in Montgomery, AL, I and others who were a part of our group were informed that there are to-date over 800 active hate-related groups identified in the U.S., and that this number has been on the rise since Obama's election as president.

None of this should be surprising, given the history of racism in our nation. In 1903, African-American sociologist W. E. B. DuBois pronounced that the problem of the 20th century would be the problem of the color-line (*The Souls of Black Folk*). In 1944, Swedish sociologist Gunnar Myrdal discussed the plight of African Americans within the context of the concomitant images of what he referred to as an "American dilemma" and the "Negro problem." (*An American Dilemma: The Negro Problem and Modern Democracy).* And in 1968, the Kerner Commission Report, based on a study which President Lyndon B. Johnson had requested in light of the civil unrest and riots that had broken out in several cities across the United States, summarized the state of race relations in America by noting that "America is a nation of two societies, one black and one white, separate and unequal."

Interestingly, Obama's campaign and election as president served to offer a vivid snapshot of the state of race relations in society today. Much of the political discourse leading up to the election focused on Obama's race and whether the nation was ready for a black president. Also interestingly, these questions were raised almost 400 years after the first African slaves arrived on what would become America's shores, and almost 150 years after the legal emancipation of slaves in America.

It is also interesting that throughout his campaign for president, Obama's qualifications for the presidency were called into question because of his choice – after graduating from Columbia University and Harvard Law School (and serving as editor of the Harvard Law Review) – to return to Chicago's south side to work as a community organizer. That he chose not to go to Wall Street, but to serve on "Main Street" with Ivy League law credentials in hand was troubling to some. The political discourse surrounding Obama as to what makes one qualified and ready for the presidency of the United States pointed to the critical choices that some have made to provide service and leadership in our cities and among the poor, often at the apparent expense of career upward mobility and professional prestige.

It is clear today that race continues to matter in America, and that we are not yet at the place of being post-racial or post-racist. This is the matter that Michael Eric Dyson addresses in his book, *Can You Hear Me Now?* Dyson insists that the critical question that is before society today is not if we are yet a *post-racial* society and the question is not even if we should strive to become post-racial, but the question is how might we move closer to becoming a *post-racist* society?

In his book, *The Audacity of Hope* (2006), then-Senator Barack Obama, offered words of caution to America in thinking that we may have arrived at becoming "post-racial" or that we already live in a color-blind society, and that we may be beyond the need for discourse and critical engagement as it regards racism and related forms of oppression and injustice. He wrote:

> To say that we are one people is not to suggest that race no longer matters – that the fight for equality has been won, or that the problems that minorities face in this country today are largely self-inflicted. We know the statistics: On almost every single socioeconomic indicator, from infant mortality to life expectancy to employment to home ownership, black and Latino Americans in particular lag far behind their white counterparts. (Obama, 232)

Politics, Religion and Hope in Changing Times

We also recall that a good deal of the political discourse during the 2008 presidential primaries focused on then-Senator Barack Obama's membership at Trinity United Church of Christ in Chicago, and his 20 year relationship with Rev. Dr. Jeremiah Wright, that church's pastor. On the surface, many of the concerns levied against Obama in light of his relationship with Wright centered on comments that Wright had made in several sermons in which he offered pointed, and what some considered to have been derogatory critiques of America and the Bush Administration in the aftermath of the 2001 terrorist attacks and in light of the current war in Iraq.

In light of Jeremiah Wright's role as a prophetic leader in the church and community for over thirty years, perhaps then it is not coincidental that like Wright, who in 2007 expressed his opposition to the war in Iraq, Rev. Dr. Martin Luther King, Jr., (40 years prior) on April 4, 1967 at Riverside Church in New York City – in a sermon entitled, "Beyond Vietnam" – similarly expressed in very vehement terms his opposition to the war in Vietnam. King stated:

> The bombs of Vietnam explode at home; they destroy the hopes and possibilities for a decent America... The war in Vietnam is but a symptom of a far deeper malady within the American spirit, and if we ignore this sobering reality, we will find ourselves organizing "clergy and laymen concerned" for the

> next generation… Now it should be incandescently clear that no one who has any concern for the integrity and life of America today can ignore the present war. If America's soul becomes totally poisoned, part of the autopsy must read "Vietnam."

King further intimated that there are real spiritual and social costs that are born as a result of war. He said:

> A nation that continues year after year to spend more money on military defense than on programs of social uplift is approaching spiritual death. America, the richest and most powerful nation in the world, can well lead the way in this revolution of values. There is nothing, except a tragic death wish, to prevent us from reordering our priorities, so that the pursuit of peace will take precedence over the pursuit of war. There is nothing to keep us from molding a recalcitrant status quo with bruised hands until we have fashioned it into a brotherhood.

Near the end of his life, King, published a book entitled, *Where Do We Go from Here: Chaos or Community?* In it, he reiterated a point he had made on several other occasions. He pointed out that we are faced with a choice in our life together, and that we will either learn to live together as sisters and brothers, or we will die together as fools.

A part of the moral prerogative of churches, civil and human rights organizations and all other institutions, and persons concerned about the well-being of our world today remains that of speaking truthfully to the critical moral and social issues of the contemporary age. It is our task to help devise and articulate a framework for engaging in critical and constructive advocacy for the disinherited among us – the poor, the violated, the marginalized and the oppressed.

And an important aspect of the churches' prophetic task is also to be self-critical as it pertains to issues such as the proliferation of the prosperity gospel, the lack of activism in many circles, the inability or unwillingness of the churches today to speak and act prophetically on matters of contemporary concern such as the war in Iraq, the widening gap between the rich and the poor in America and around the world, the ongoing proliferation of racial (and other forms of) bigotry, the marginalization of too many in our society, along with the generally violent and misogynous nature of hip hop and other expressions of popular culture.

Finding Hope in the Midst of Despair

Where might hope reside among all people as we look to the future? Rev. Dr. Martin Luther King, Jr., framed his vision of hope within the context of *Beloved Community*. In one of his later sermons, "The Meaning of Hope," he defined hope as that quality which is "necessary for life." (see Baker-Fletcher, 1993, 132)

King asserted that hope was to be viewed as "animated and undergirded by faith and love." In his mind, if you had hope, you had faith in something. Thus, hope shares the belief that "all reality hinges on moral foundations." (Baker-Fletcher)

"The hopeless individual is the dead individual." In King's view hope had a transformative quality that keeps human beings "alive" both spiritually and psychologically. (Baker-Fletcher) Hope, therefore, is "one of the basic structures of an adequate life."

For King, hope was the refusal to give up "despite overwhelming odds." Hope beckons us to love everybody – both our enemies and allies. Hope helps us to see that we can resist giving up on one another because our lives together are animated by the belief that God is present in each and every one of us.

In the third century, Augustine, the Bishop of Hippo intimated that "Hope has two beautiful daughters; their names are Anger and Courage. Anger at the way things are, and Courage to see that they do not remain the way they are."

Is There No Balm?

"For surely, I know the plans I have for you, says the Lord, plans for your welfare (shalom, wholeness), and not for your harm, plans to give you a future with hope." (Jeremiah 29:11)

The prophet Jeremiah offers a vision of hope for a people experiencing exile in a strange city. In the sixth century B.C.E., the Israelites were in Babylon – alienated from their land, alienated from their God, and alienated – many of them - from their loved ones.

We can imagine that the Israelites experienced what some philosophers have come to refer to as a certain nihilism – where a certain nothingness, meaninglessness, lovelessness, and hopelessness comes to define the existence of a people. It is against this backdrop of existential nihilism that Jeremiah shares these words of hope:

> *"For surely, I know the plans I have for you, says the Lord, plans for your welfare (shalom, wholeness, well-being), and not for your harm, plans to give you a future with hope." (Jeremiah 29:11)*

Certainly, hope could have been a fleeting, abstract concept in times like those in which Jeremiah wrote. Those were the same times and conditions that would lead the psalmist to write other familiar words of these people in exile –

> *"By the rivers of Babylon – there we sat and we wept when we remembered Zion. And our captors asked us to sing to them the songs of Zion... How can we sing the Lord's song in a strange land?" (Psalm 137:1-4)*

And those were the same times that would lead Jeremiah earlier in his writing to offer provocative questions to the same people –

"Is there no balm in Gilead? Is there no healing there? Why then has the health of my people not been restored?" (Jer. 8:22)

Perhaps the context in which Jeremiah wrote is not much unlike that of our days. In many ways hope today seems fleeting - with political unrest, social disarray, family distress, community disintegration and economic uncertainty.

Is there no balm in Gilead? In reflecting on this text, Dr. Martin Luther King, Jr. pointed out that the evidence of faith and hope is found in the fact that persons were able to convert the *question marks* of the prophet Jeremiah's lament, into *exclamation points* as they affirmed their faith and hope in a living and life-giving God in a song:

There is a balm in Gilead,
To make the wounded whole.
There is a balm in Gilead,
To heal the sin-sick soul.
Sometimes I feel discouraged
And think my work's in vain.
And then the Holy Spirit
Revives my soul again! (see *Songs of Zion*, 123)

Holding onto Hope

Hope can be found in the possibilities that we will continue to discover ways to capitalize on those experiences and encounters that will lead to us being intentional and inclusive community. This is the hope that must be realized if we are to be the *Beloved Community* that King imagined.

In the days ahead, may we continue to conjure the audacity to dream dreams and see visions, may we have the temerity to hope against all that seems to rise against hope, and may we forever have the courage to hold onto hope.

-4-
DARE TO DREAM

(This sermon was preached at First Baptist Church, Chillicothe, OH, January 16, 2011.)

"And afterward, I will pour out my Spirit on all people. Your sons and daughters will prophesy, your men will dream dreams, your young will see visions. Even on my servants, both men and women, I will pour out my Spirit in those days. I will show wonders in the heavens and on the earth, blood and fire and billows of smoke. The sun will be turned to darkness and the moon to blood before the coming of the great and dreadful day of the LORD. And everyone who calls on the name of the LORD will be saved; for on Mount Zion and in Jerusalem there will be deliverance, as the LORD has said, even among the survivors whom the LORD calls. (Joel 2:28-32)

In the reading from the book of the prophet Joel, it is written, *"And it shall come to pass, afterward, that I will pour out my Spirit on all flesh; and your sons and daughters shall prophesy; your old men (and women) shall dream dreams, your young men (and women) shall see visions."* (Joel 2:28)

How fitting it is that we hear these words this weekend as we celebrate the life and legacy of the Rev. Dr. Martin Luther King, Jr. I believe that if Dr. King was anything, he was a dreamer and a visionary, a man chosen by God to be a prophet in our midst.

We recall that in our nation's capital almost 48 years ago, Dr. King shared his dream and what he envisioned for our world. We recall that he dreamt of a world where the descendants of former slaves and former slave-owners would be able to sit down together at the table of brotherhood… a world where little children would someday live in a nation where they would not be judged by the color of their skin, but by the content of their character.

Dr. King envisioned a world where we would grow to see the face of God in Native Americans, Asians, Hispanics, Whites, Blacks, Jews, Muslims, Buddhists, Hindus, Catholics and Protestants, and people from all other racial, ethnic, social, cultural or religious backgrounds. He dared to dream and envision:

- A world of peace and love among all women and men, girls and boys…
- A world where we would study war no more…
- A world where poverty, hunger and homelessness would be eradicated…
- A world where violence and abuse would exist no longer.

And it's sad to say that Dr. King's dreams and visions – those same dreams and visions that cost him his life have - in many respects – gone unfulfilled and unrealized, and find themselves in sea of despair and brokenness throughout our world today.

In the midst of this, it often seems that, for whatever reasons, we have lost our ability to dream. In too many places, hopelessness seems to abound. Indeed, despair and what Dr. Cornel West calls a certain "nihilism" seems to be pervasive among us – where a certain meaninglessness, lovelessness, nothingness and hopelessness seems to permeate our collective reality.

In fact, toward the conclusion of his life, Dr. King wondered out loud about the dream he had articulated for America and the world in August 1963, and whether or not his dream had become a "nightmare." In 1967, he stated, "I must confess that the dream that I had that day has in many points turned into nightmare. Now I'm not one to lose hope, I keep on hoping. I still have faith in the future. But I have had to analyze many things over the last few years and I would say over the last few months."

This leads us to ask ourselves the questions, "What has really happened to King's dream? What has happened to our own ability to hope and love and envision and dream? Where are our dreams and visions today?"

- Have we forgotten how to dream?
- Have we forgotten that it was God almighty – God omnipotent and omniscient – who in the beginning created the world – "ex nihilo" – out of nothing?
- Have we forgotten that it was God who delivered God's people out of the bondage of their lives amidst Egyptian slavery?
- Have we forgotten that with God there is really no such thing as nihilism (nothingness), for God is always up to something in our lives? God is always working to make something out of nothing in our lives.

- Have we forgotten that it is God who beckons us to dare to dream and envision what our tomorrows will be?

And so the word of hope – the word from the Lord today is that we can and should all be dreamers and visionaries. We can and should dare to dream. If we need more encouragement, we have evidence throughout history of God calling forth dreamers.

- Joseph, the youngest son of Jacob, was a dreamer. He dreamt of a different future for his life and that of his family and his nation.
- David dreamt of a community of faith that would love God with their whole heart and praise God at all times.
- Peter was a dreamer, who we find in the book of Acts preaching to the early church, sharing the same dream and vision of the prophet Joel, where in the last day, God would pour out God's spirit on all flesh, and older persons would dream dreams, and younger persons would see visions.
- And Jesus dreamt. Jesus prophetically challenged the people of his day to envision a world where the presence of the Lord – the kin-dom of God - had been ushered in, a world where the salvation of God - the wholeness, blessedness and peace of God was evident and alive for all humanity.

And Dr. King came in a similar manner not only to dream himself, but to prophetically challenge each of us to dare, in our heart of hearts, to dream and envision a better world, knowing that through faith and hope, and steadfastness and courage, we could live a better tomorrow. He dared to dream.

Dr. Benjamin Elijah Mays, one of Dr. King's mentors at Morehouse College also spoke to the importance of dreaming. "The tragedy in life doesn't lie in not reaching a goal. The tragedy lies in having no goal to reach. It isn't a calamity to die with dreams unfulfilled, but it is a calamity not to dream. It is not a disgrace not to reach the stars, but it is a disgrace to have no stars to reach for. Not failure, but low aim is sin."

The poet Langston Hughes likewise dared to dream. In his seminal poem "I Dream a World!", Hughes shared:

> I dream a world where no man
> No other man will scorn,
> Where love will bless the earth
> And peace its path adorn.
> I dream a world where all
> Will know sweet freedom's way,
> Where greed no longer saps the soul
> Nor avarice blights the day.
> A world I dream where black or white,
> Whatever race you be,
> Will share the bounties of the earth
> And every man is free,
> Where wretchedness will hang its head
> And joy, like pearl,
> Attends the needs of all mankind-
> Of such I dream my world!

There's the story of an eagle. As it was nested and born, the eagle by chance found itself growing up among a group of prairie chickens. The eagle learned to live like a prairie chicken; it ate like a prairie chicken; it moved like a prairie chicken; it even tried to quack like a prairie chicken. And the eagle never learned to fly.

As the eagle grew older, it realized that there was something that made it different from the prairie chickens that it had grown up with. The eagle's wings began to expand, and it had the urge to fly. One day, the eagle's owner realized that the eagle was about to fly off, and decided to clip the eagle's wings so that it could not fly away. And so the eagle never realized that it was an eagle, and continued to live as a prairie chicken – unable to fly - for the rest of its life.

Too many of us today continue to see ourselves as (and act like) prairie chickens.
Too many of us never come to realize that we can fly like eagles.

In another of his poems, Langston Hughes encourages us:

Hold fast to dreams
For if dreams die
Life is a broken-winged bird
That cannot fly.

We can and should dare to dream. The good news is that through faithful people like you and me, Dr. King's dreams can become reality in this present day. His dreams can come alive:

- As we advocate and work to address poverty and oppression,
- As we continue to fight for healthcare for everybody,
- As we commit ourselves to peace with justice for all humanity,
- As we work for a nonviolent society,
- As we hold before ourselves the belief in the words etched in our Declaration of Independence, that "all (people) are created equal"... And therefore all people are free to go where they want to go, live where they want to live, eat where they want to eat, be educated where they want to be educated, and work where they want to work.

Indeed, we are called today to dare to dream - to dream dreams and see visions. Dare to dream of what our families (and our young people)... and our churches... and our communities... and our governments... and our world will be in the days to come. Dare to dream.

How might this come to be? This is possible because the God of eternity and grace is not dead and not done. With God all things are possible. Jesus lives! And as long as Jesus lives – lives in you and me - our dreams and visions shall not die.

-5-

AN ADVENT MEDITATION ON HOPE

For those of us who walk by faith, this is the season of hope, and hope is embedded, embodied, intertwined and entangled in the life of Jesus –

Hope came to the earth in the form of God's own and only son.
Hope came as Love wrapped up in flesh.
Hope was conceived in an unwed teenage mother. Hope had an earthly father who was a working class man. He was a carpenter.
Hope came into the world of moderate means – if not poor.
Hope had the odds stacked against Him.
Hope came as the Prince of Peace.
Hope came as Joy to the World.
Hope came – fully divine.
Hope came fully human – just like you and me.
Hope came to let us know that God is with us, and in some ways God is like us, and God knows us.
Hope came to save the world, and to let us know that because He's hope, there's nothing that we should be hopeless about today or tomorrow.

-6-

THESE STONES

(This sermon was preached at Epworth Chapel United Methodist Church in Baltimore in February 2013.)

When the entire nation had finished crossing over the Jordan, the Lord said to Joshua: "Select twelve men from the people, one from each tribe, and command them, 'Take twelve stones from here out of the middle of the Jordan, from the place where the priests' feet stood, carry them over with you, and lay them down in the place where you camp tonight.'" Then Joshua summoned the twelve men from the Israelites, whom he had appointed, one from each tribe. Joshua said to them, "Pass on before the ark of the Lord your God into the middle of the Jordan, and each of you take up a stone on his shoulder, one for each of the tribes of the Israelites, so that this may be a sign among you. When your children ask in time to come, 'What do these stones mean to you?' then you shall tell them that the waters of the Jordan were cut off in front of the ark of the covenant of the Lord. When it crossed over the Jordan, the waters of the Jordan were cut off. So these stones shall be to the Israelites a memorial forever." (Joshua 4:1-7)

Somebody once said, "Humanity is at a great crossroads. One path leads to despair and utter alienation, and the other leads to destruction of all that we hold dear." On the face of it, this is a rather morbid, hopeless proposition, but it really leads us to think about life and where we are today.

Indeed, we face many crossroads of life today. Society's problems are numerous and complex. The choices that we must make, both individually and collectively are choices that can lead – if they are not the right choices – to the obliteration of the land at worst, or at the very least, to some demise of our minds, bodies and spirits.

At these crossroads of life, God's people are asking "how do we overcome the senselessness in our midst – senseless violence, senseless wars, perpetual poverty, illiteracy, broken homes, race division, and apparent hopelessness all around us/"

At these crossroads, we are led to wonder what God has in store for us. What does the future hold for us? Where do we go from here? And how in the world are we going to make it there?

We can imagine that this is how the Israelites felt. They had just crossed over to the other side of the Jordan River after a 40 year journey in the wilderness. And they didn't know what the future held for them. In Joshua 4, twelve stones are placed to remind the Israelites of where they had been, that it was God who had made a way for their deliverance, and that they should never forget from whence they had come.

Stones are – on the face of things – a rather mundane part of creation. We see them every day but probably don't pay much attention. They come in every shape and dimension. They can be larger or smaller. Though rather mundane, stones are ubiquitous among us, we find them in water and on mountains. We find them in cities and in fields. They don't seem to have a great deal of relevance in and of themselves.

I once served as the pastor of a church whose membership included a number of stone-builders. These persons used stones to build homes (even some for the rich and famous) and even the church in which we worshipped. These stone-builders took pride in their work, and in their intricate, intimate knowledge of stones. All stones to them were not created equally. In fact, I learned that each and every stone was peculiar, and was uniquely created.

We find in the book of Joshua that stones are central to the crossing over narrative in our text. In the Hebrew context, the word "stone" represented a sacred object. The Hebrew word for stone, transliterated is *`eben* which is continuously mentioned in this chapter. Perhaps the initial significance of stones in Scripture is seen through Moses, who received the law and the Ten Commandments from God on tablets of stone (Exodus 24:12) for the purpose of teaching and guiding the people.

Here, Joshua is depicted as the new Moses. Just as Moses carried the role of prophet and priest, so would Joshua carry such important roles for the people. As Israel journeyed toward the Promised Land, this occurrence signifies that God has surely remained with them. The crossing over the Jordan serves as witness of God's enduring presence and promise. As the ark of the covenant of the Lord was in their possession during this incredible passage, this story also stands to show the awesome provision, protection and power of God.

And they were instructed to select and to lay down 12 stones. The stones were laid for the purpose of remembering what had taken place at Gilgal for the twelve tribes of Israel, but also to share that the river had ceased flowing. These two remarkable events were to be memorialized for all the generations who would follow. The stones symbolized that the location where they were placed was holy ground; they were sacred objects placed as a memorial. These stones were special remembrances of what their ancestors had lived through.

Indeed, these stones would serve as reminders of all the struggles, trials, tribulations, tears and toil that God's people had encountered and endured in getting to the place where God wanted them to be.

To "remember" was an important ritual and spiritual discipline in the life of the Israelites. To "remember" in the Hebrew language meant not only to recall what had occurred in the past, but to experience the past, and to learn from the past the lessons that would make for a better future. Remembering was important not only for the present generation, but for the generations to come.

The Israelites were people of memories – of "remembering." Every year, they would gather to celebrate and remember – at the Passover – how God had blessed them, protected them and delivered them. Passover, more than anything was a time of sharing memories.

They would remember how they had suffered and struggled, how God had brought them through their wandering, through 430 years of Egyptian slavery, through plagues, and through Pharaoh's persecution. They would remember how God had parted the Red Sea and set them free, how God had brought them through 40 years of wilderness wandering, and now how God had brought them to the point of their promise.

They didn't forget that through it all, God had been good to them, and had brought them from a mighty long way.

One of the things that we seem to lack today – even as people of faith – is the ability to remember. It seems that in our busy-ness and striving to move forward in life, we've too often forgotten to take time to remember from whence we have come, and to recognize how we got to where we are in life. It is a particularly dangerous predicament for our children and the generations that will come after them not to know and remember from whence they have come. Because when we fail to remember, we face the real risks that generations that are to come will have no real bearings; they will have nothing to remember because memories were never passed to them.

And so, for the Israelites, these 12 stones would serve as markers for them. These stones would serve to help them remember. They would stand not merely as the stones themselves, but as something much more. They would serve as points of hope and possibility - for in light of what God had done, they knew that God had more blessings in store for them.

Dr. Martin Luther King, Jr. shared his hope for the nation and the world on the steps of the Lincoln Memorial in 1963, when he shared that he dreamed that God would hew out to the "mountain of despair (among us) a stone of hope."

The Israelite's 12 stones were to be stones of hope. What are some of the stones of remembrance that we should hold onto today? What are the ways that God has blessed us and never left us? How has God delivered us and made ways where there seemed to be no way? How has God been our joy in sorrow and our hope for tomorrow?

We are encouraged to see these – all of these - as stones of remembrance, stones of hope for today, and for all of the days that will come.

-7-

HOPE IN CHANGING TIMES

(This lecture was delivered at St. Mary's Seminary and University in November 2009 at the Fall Open House/Convocation for the Ecumenical Institute of Theology.)

These are days of tremendous change and challenge in our society. From the collapse of the economy that has affected all of us – to the wars that are now being fought in at least two places in the Middle East – to the proliferation of violence that affects many of our urban communities - to the healthcare crisis that has resulted in over 40 million Americans living without adequate healthcare today, these are days of unprecedented change and challenge.

These are days that beckon the church to seek out ways to articulate and appropriate hope that speaks to such despair and change. As a Christian theologian, hope is one of primary areas in which I am called to trade on a consistent, persistent basis. For me, a critical question for us to address today is one posed by theologian Howard Thurman in his 1949 book *Jesus and the Disinherited*, "What does the life of Jesus of Nazareth have to say to persons whose backs are against the wall?" (Thurman, 11)

One theologian who has been instrumental in helping the Christian church arrive at a way of talking about hope is Jürgen Moltmann. In his book, *Theology of Hope* Moltmann offers an eschatologically-centered perspective on hope that focuses on the hope that the Resurrection brings. According to him, through faith we are bound to Christ, and as such we have the hope of the resurrected Christ, and can anticipate his return. For Moltmann, the hope of the Christian faith is hope in the resurrection of Christ crucified. Hope and faith depend on each other to remain true and substantial; and only with both may one find "not only a consolation in suffering, but also the protest of the divine promise against suffering." (Moltmann, 1993, 19-20)

Hope strengthens faith, helps believers live lives of love, and directs us toward a new creation of all things. It creates in us a "passion for the possible." "For our knowledge and comprehension of reality, and our reflections on it, that means at least this: that in the medium of hope our theological concepts become not judgments which nail reality down to what it is, but anticipations which show reality its prospects and its future possibilities." (Moltmann, 22)

One of my primary concerns is exploring ways of explicating and appropriating Christian hope within the context of the oppression experienced by many African Americans, Latina/os, Native Americans and others disparately impacted by racism, classism and poverty in America and abroad, both historically and contemporarily. Here, mine is an effort to offer a constructive contextualization of theology within the context of a broader theological discourse.

Here, we are reminded of another thought from Howard Thurman, that "any text without a context is a pretext." And again, the question that Thurman raised in *Jesus and the Disinherited* is critical, "What does the life of Jesus of Nazareth have to say to persons who have their backs against the wall?"

In one of his later sermons, "The Meaning of Hope," Dr. Martin Luther King, Jr. defined hope as that quality which is "necessary for life." (Baker-Fletcher, 232)

King asserted that hope was to be viewed as "animated and undergirded by faith and love." In his mind, if you had hope, you had faith in something. Thus, hope shares the belief that "all reality hinges on moral foundations." (Baker-Fletcher)

For King, hope was the refusal to give up "despite overwhelming odds." This hope beckons us to love everybody – both our enemies and allies. This hope helps us to see that we can resist giving up on one another because our lives together are animated by the belief that God is present in each and every one of us.

In his famous "I Have a Dream" speech delivered in our nation's capital in the summer of 1963, King shared that a part of his dream was that we would be able "to hew out of the mountain of despair, a stone of hope."

Barack Obama and Hope Renewed

At the historic election of Barack Obama as the 44th President of the United States last November, many people seemed to sense (and hope) that his election had ushered in an age of post-racism and post-racialism in America – and perhaps around the world. A year later, we discover as a nation that we are continuing to come to grips with the racial and racist realities that have and continue to afflict us.

We recall that in a major address entitled "A More Perfect Union", delivered during his presidential campaign, Obama offered an analysis of the prevalence of racial tensions which have continued to define the relationship between the black and white communities in America. Obama argued that to simply shelve anger or "wish it away" (the race problem in America) could prove to be completely detrimental. Unambiguously, Obama pointed to a belief that race factors into the opportunities provided to each American citizen.

To support his assertion, he noted that the inferior school systems today are often the ones that were segregated fifty years ago. Obama shared that the history of racism in America is undeniably at the root of the lack of opportunities for African Americans today. In light of this, it is both achievable and necessary for all Americans to unite and battle racial prejudices and oppression. According to Obama, in order to move to a "more perfect union", people of all races need to recognize the historically oppressive and tyrannical nature of racism and its impact on the black experience in America.

Indeed there are considerable challenges to arriving at a hope that is fully realized. In 1992, philosopher Cornel West authored an important book entitled, *Race Matters.* The book was written against the backdrop of the Los Angeles riots of April 1992, which followed the acquittal of the police officers charged in the beating of Rodney King, and the ensuing racial tensions in that city. In the book, West pointed to what he referred to as the "nihilism of Black America" – where a certain nothingness, meaninglessness, lovelessness and hopelessness seemed to have pervaded and permeated much of our society – particularly in the urban context, and as it pertains to Black and Brown people. According to West at that time, race mattered in America, and we as a society must continue to attend to matters of race.

In his more recent book *Hope on a Tightrope* (2008) West cautions against a false sense of security in hope, yet unborn. He points out that real hope is grounded in a particularly messy struggle and it can be betrayed by naive projections of a better future that ignore the necessity of doing real work. For West, real hope is closely connected to attributes like courage, faith, freedom and wisdom. It comes out of a history of struggle, and points to a future filled with the possibilities of promise and progress.

Here we are reminded of the sentiments of persons like:

- Frederick Douglas who, in his call for the abolition of slavery in America, intimated that progress never comes about without struggle.

- Fannie Lou Hamer, the Mississippi share-cropper who led the fight for voting rights for persons across the south, and reminded persons that progress comes through perseverance even when we are "sick and tired of being sick and tired."
- Mohandas K. Gandhi who in the midst of the revolutionary struggle for the freedom of the people of India reminded them that they had to become the change that they sought in the world.
- Dietrich Bonhoeffer, the German Lutheran theologian who engaged in the struggle to end the atrocities of Hitler's Nazism, and reminded us that Christian discipleship calls us to practice a costly form of grace.
- Desmond Tutu, who led the fight against South African Apartheid, and its related racial/ethnic atrocities.

Hope and the Beloved Community Revisited

Near the end of his life, Rev. Dr. Martin Luther King, Jr. published a book entitled, *Where Do We Go from Here: Chaos or Community?* In it, King reiterated a point he had made on several other occasions. He pointed out that we are faced with a choice in our life together, and that we will either learn to live together as brothers and sisters, or we will die together as fools.

Hope for a better future is ultimately rooted and grounded in our shared potential to change the world. The church and society of today look quite different from the church and society of forty years ago. Progress can be seen in many areas. And yet there is still much work that lies ahead of us.

My hope is rooted and grounded in the possibility that we will continue to discover ways to capitalize on those experiences and encounters that will lead us to becoming an inclusive and authentic community. This is the hope that must be realized if we are to be the church, the *Beloved Community*, which Christ calls us to become.

Finally, Dr. King shared that everybody can be great because everybody can serve. He further shared that our service is the rent that we pay for the space that we occupy here on earth. My prayer is that each of us in the days ahead would recommit ourselves to paying some rent.

-8-

HOPE IN HARD TIMES

GOD'S ANSWER TO THE HEALTHCARE CRISIS

(This article was originally published on my blog at www.newurbanminstryblogspot.com in July 2009.)

Recently, in one of the graduate seminary courses that I teach, the question was raised within the context of a discussion on social justice and civil rights about whether anyone in the group had recently heard a sermon dealing with the current healthcare crisis facing our nation. In the room there was a collective silence – none could recall having heard - or having preached - such a sermon. This is particularly interesting in light of the constant media coverage today focusing on the struggles facing President Barack Obama and his anadministration in moving forward with a comprehensive plan to reform our nation's healthcare system and provide affordable access to coverage for the more than 40 million Americans who do not now have adequate coverage – most of whom are women and children. Also among this number are a disproportionate number of Brown and Black persons – and those living in urban and rural areas.

The response of this group of students led me to wonder what God has to say about the current healthcare crisis facing us. In the 7th century B.C.E., the Prophet Jeremiah posed a series of questions to the Israelites:

"Is there no balm in Gilead; is there no physician there? Why then has the health of my poor people not been restored?" (Jeremiah 8:22)

These questions were raised in light of the experience of exile and pain among the people of Israel. The region of Gilead was known for producing a healing balm. This balm was known for its medicinal powers. When people were hurting, they would seek out the balm from Gilead, for it was like no other in its ability to facilitate healing. The balm from Gilead was considered to be a miracle cure; if it couldn't heal one's wounds, there was perhaps nothing that would.

Jeremiah spoke to the Israelites who found themselves dealing with brokenness and alienation from God, brokenness and alienation from their land, brokenness and alienation from their possessions, and brokenness and alienation from one another. And the questions that the prophet poses in light of this serve as a reminder of God's will of mercy and justice for and among God's people.

Later in the book of Jeremiah, the prophet again offers a reminder of God's will in light of concerns about brokenness and dis-ease. Jeremiah encourages the people to *"seek the welfare of the city where I have sent you into exile, and pray to the Lord on its behalf, for in its welfare you will find your welfare... For surely I know the plans I have for you, says the Lord, plans for your welfare and not for harm, to give you a future with hope."* (Jeremiah 29:7, 11)

Jeremiah's reminder of God's will and concern for the welfare of those in the city (and the suburbs and rural areas) has significance and implications for the church and society today. "Welfare" in the context which Jeremiah speaks on behalf of God has broader connotations than our common usage of the term. It speaks to wholeness, wellness, peace (shalom), health and healing (and by extension healthcare). Indeed, it is clear that God wills for the health(care) of God's people.

Rev. Dr. Martin Luther King, Jr. reminded us that "true peace is not merely the absence of tension; it is the presence of justice." May God inspire us to speak and act with grace, mercy and justice in light of those who are broken and hurting among us. May we live the prayer of Rev. Ted Loder in "Strengthen Us to Answer with Brave Hearts" -

God of grace,
As you did with Rosa Parks and Martin Luther King, Jr.,
Mother Teresa, Nelson Mandela and Desmond Tutu,
strengthen us to answer with brave hearts, your call to help
shape a world, not of death and oppression, but of life and
hope.

-9 -

BEYOND AFGHANISTAN: MARTIN LUTHER KING, JR. and REFLECTIONS on WAR and PEACE

(This commentary was published in the United Methodist Connection of the Baltimore-Washington Conference in January 2010.)

In this, the year of the 81st anniversary of the birth of Rev. Dr. Martin Luther King, Jr., we pause to reflect on the state of our nation and world, and the prospects of peace among us. On December 1, 2009 President Barack Obama shared with the nation his decision to increase American troop levels in Afghanistan by 30,000 over the next six months, with plans for the withdrawal of American troops by the end of 2011. President Obama, whose presidential ambitions were launched, in no small way, based upon his stated opposition to the war in Iraq, indicated that the rationale for the troop expansion in Afghanistan was based on an increased sense of urgency to conclude the war begun in the immediate aftermath of terrorist attacks on America on September 11, 2001.

What would Dr. Martin Luther King, Jr. have to say about the current war in Afghanistan – and President Obama's decision? Perhaps the best indicator can be found in King's comments on the War in Vietnam. On April 4, 1967 at Riverside Church in New York City – in a sermon entitled, "Beyond Vietnam" – King expressed in very vehement terms his opposition to the war in Vietnam. He began by stating that "there comes a time when silence is betrayal." He went on to state, "The bombs in Vietnam explode at home, they destroy the hopes and possibilities for a decent America… The war in Vietnam is but a symptom of a far deeper malady within the American spirit, and if we ignore this sobering reality, we will find ourselves organizing 'clergy and laymen concerned' for the next generation... Now it should be incandescently clear that no one who has any concern for the integrity and life of America today can ignore the present war. If America's soul becomes totally poisoned, part of the autopsy must read: 'Vietnam'."

In "Beyond Vietnam," King intimated that there are real spiritual, moral and social costs that are born as a result of war. He said, "A nation that continues year after year to spend more money on military defense than on programs of social uplift is approaching spiritual death. America, the richest and most powerful nation in the world, can well lead the way in this revolution of values. There is nothing, except a tragic death wish, to prevent us from reordering our priorities, so that the pursuit of peace will take precedence over the pursuit of war. There is nothing to keep us from molding a recalcitrant status quo with bruised hands until we have fashioned it into a brotherhood."

In April 2003, I published an essay entitled, "Counting the Costs: Reflections on the Church and Just War" on the brink of the decision of President George W. Bush and his administration to engage in war with Iraq. I wrote then that it seemed appropriate for the church to continue to consider (and reconsider) the matter of the justice of war from both philosophical and Christian perspectives. In terms of the morality of war, those who have thought, written and acted on such matters have historically raised particular questions as it pertains to the determinants of when war might be justified. In the fifth century, St. Augustine, the Christian philosopher and theologian, was instrumental in the development of seven criteria for determining whether or not a war is "just." First, there must exist a just cause. The war must confront an unquestioned danger. Second, competent authority must exist. The leader committing a nation to war must be acting on behalf of his/her people. Third, there should be right intention. The reasons set forth should be the actual objectives, and retaliation must not be the aim. Fourth, war should be the last resort. All peaceful alternatives must have been exhausted. Fifth, there needs to be the probability of success. Sixth, discrimination requires the immunity of noncombatants from direct attack. And seventh, the good that will be achieved by war cannot be outweighed by the harm that is done.

In light of the general philosophical criteria outlined here, particular concerns exist as to how these can be applied to the U.S. wars in Iraq and Afghanistan. Specifically, have the alleged atrocities of Saddam Hussein (in Iraq) and the Taliban (in Afghanistan) warranted – over the past 8 years - the killing and maiming of countless innocent women, men and children? This is not to speak of the annihilation of an untold number of Iraqi and Afghani buildings, homes, shopping malls, factories, schools, and places of worship.

In 2003, I wrote that for those of us who are Christians, it seems that ours are not only philosophical concerns about whether or not a particular war is just, but our concerns center on what it means to live as disciples of Jesus Christ. And the matter of our attitudes and actions in Christ do not stop with asking the popular question, "What would Jesus do?" For it seems to be clear that Jesus did not - and would not - engage in such atrocities as the war in Iraq (or Afghanistan). The critical question for the church is also "What is Jesus doing in the lives of Christians today, and how does this lead us to respond?"

In the midst of the war in Vietnam, King stated in 1967 that, "The church must be reminded that it is not the master or the servant of the state, rather it is the conscience of the state. It must be the guide and the critic of the state, and never its tool. If the church does not recapture its prophetic zeal, it will become an irrelevant social club without moral or spiritual authority."

And so in these times where war persists in our midst, it is my sense that King would call the church as he did in 1967, yet again to reclaim its prophetic voice, and remind us that "true peace is not merely the absence of tension, it is the presence of justice, and that violence and war anywhere in the world is a threat to peace everywhere."

-10-

SUNDAY MORNING - IS IT THE MOST SEGREGATED HOUR OF THE WEEK?

(This lecture was delivered at Emmanuel Episcopal Church, Baltimore, Maryland on January 31, 2011.)

In reflecting on the matter of Sunday morning and the problem of segregation in the church (*The Problem of Sunday Morning*) - in other words in addressing the question of whether or not Sunday morning is the most segregated hour of the week - I am led to reflect on two past experiences in light of any data which might address this matter. These two experiences have had a profound impact on my thinking on the issue of the church and the race problem in America, and thus serve to shape and frame my response to this important question.

Before reflecting on these two experiences, it is important to point out that racial segregation in the churches is to be viewed against the historical backdrop of the racism in American society, in general. In 1903, African-American sociologist W. E. B. DuBois pronounced that "the problem of the 20th century is the problem of the color-line. (*The Souls of Black Folk*) And in 1944, Swedish sociologist Gunnar Myrdal discussed the plight of African Americans (the Negro Problem) within the context of what he referred to as the "American dilemma." (*An American Dilemma: The Negro Problem and Modern Democracy)*

This month on the occasion of the 82nd anniversary of the birth of the Rev. Dr. Martin Luther King, Jr., and the time of year when we celebrate the history of people of the African Diaspora in America, and two years after the historic inauguration of Barack Obama as the 44th president of the United States, several recent events serve to remind us that one of the critical problems of the 21st century in America (perhaps the most critical problem) remains the problem of the color-line. Among these events are the politically contentious 2009 Supreme Court confirmation hearings of Justice Sonia Sotomayor; the arrest of distinguished Harvard University Professor Henry Louis Gates at his home in Cambridge, MA; the emergence of the Tea Party and other right-wing factions across America who seem intent on "taking back their country"; ongoing discourse on issues related to immigration reform; and the ongoing debates surrounding President Obama's efforts to reform the nation's healthcare system.

We recall that for many people across the nation and world, Obama's historic election as the first president of African descent renewed (or birthed) a sense of hope. For many, his election seemed to point to glimmers of hope that our society had somehow arrived at our ideals of "*e pluribus unum*" (out of many one), and the creed shared in our nation's Declaration of Independence, "We hold these truths to be self-evident, that all (persons) are created equal."

Many also seemed to sense (and hope) that the election of Obama had ushered in an age of post-racialism and post-racism in America – and perhaps around the world.

Two years later, we discover that we as a nation are continuing to come to grips with the racial and racist realities that still afflict us. During a recent visit to the Southern Poverty Law Center in Montgomery, AL, I and others who were a part of the visit were informed that there were over 800 hate-related groups identified in 2008, and that this number is on the rise since Obama's election as president.

It is clear today that race continues to matter in America, and that we are not yet at the place of being post-racial or post-racist. This is the matter that Michael Eric Dyson addresses in his book, *Can You Hear Me Now?* Dyson insists that the critical question that is before society today is not if we are yet a *post-racial* society and the question is not even if we should strive to become post-racial, but the question is how might we move closer to becoming a *post-racist* society? As it regards the church and the problem of race, in many ways, a pall remains over much – if not most - of the contemporary church with regard to how it has dealt with the race problem in America. In their book, *Divided by Faith: Evangelical Religion and the Problem of Race,* Michael Emerson and Christian Smith developed a theory to explain why churches continue to be racially exclusive enclaves despite Christian ideals about being inclusive: Americans choose where and with whom to worship; race is one of the most important grounds on which they choose; so the more choice they have, the more their religious institutions will be segregated. (see Emerson and Smith, 154f.)

Through sociological analysis, Emerson and Smith tested their theory and found it to be valid. Churches are more segregated than schools, workplaces, or neighborhoods. The least segregated sector of American society is also the least governed by choice; it's the military. Because white Protestants are the largest religious community in the U.S., they have the greatest choice as to with whom to gather. The authors point out that ninety-five percent of churches are effectively racially segregated, with 80 percent or more of their members being of the same race. (Emerson and Smith)

Thus, about 5 percent of religious congregations in the U.S. can fairly be considered multicultural/multiracial, with the majority of Christians engaging in what sociologists call homophily, or the desire to congregate with "birds of the same feather," with their congregations reflecting ethnoracial particularism.

In light of these sociological phenomena and the related statistics, I believe that the two personal experiences that I referred to earlier may shed additional light on the matter of Sunday morning and racial segregation.

Both of these experiences were study trips to Alabama that I was privileged to lead/teach in 2006 and 2009. On both of these occasions, groups of about 20 doctoral students and faculty from Wesley Theological Seminary traveled through Birmingham, Montgomery and Selma, Alabama retracing the steps of those who participated in the American Civil Rights movement in the 1950's and 60's.

On both occasions, the groups of participants were very diverse. We were women and men; Whites, African Americans, Caribbeans, Native Americans, Hispanics and Asians. We were from several different Christian denominations: United Methodist, Baptist, African Methodist Episcopal, African Methodist Episcopal Zion, and Episcopal.

We began each day with singing, praying and reading Scripture, as was the practice in the tradition of those who participated in the Civil Rights movement in the 1960's. John Lewis, now a U.S. Congressman, and one who labored on the front lines of the movement, has intimated that "We never went out without singing and praying." And so before leaving each morning, those of us on these doctoral immersion trips prayed, read Scripture, and sang freedom songs like "Oh Freedom," "We Shall Overcome," "There is a Balm" and "Ain't Gonna Let Nobody Turn Me Around".

As we traveled, reflected and listened together - struggling through many of the difficult paths and realities of those who lived the Civil Rights movement - we sensed among ourselves the real possibility that culturally inclusive community - *Beloved Community* - could indeed be realized in our lifetime.

We visited and studied at numerous sites that were significant to the Civil Rights movement of the 1950's and 60's. In Montgomery, we visited Dexter Avenue King Memorial Baptist Church, where Rev. Dr. Martin Luther King, Jr. served as pastor from 1954-1960 at the height of the Montgomery Bus Boycott and other significant Civil

Rights events. Just two blocks from Dexter Avenue Church, we visited the First Confederate White House - the home of Jefferson Davis, the president of the Confederacy. Sitting between Dexter Avenue Church and the first Confederate White House is the Alabama State Capitol – the place where Governor George Wallace and other state officials stood in defiance of any efforts towards integration and equal rights among the races, and where Wallace was noted to have exclaimed, "Segregation now, segregation tomorrow, segregation forever."

In Birmingham, one of the places we visited was the Sixteenth Street Baptist Church, which on September 15, 1963 was bombed by segregationists, and where four black girls were killed in the church basement while preparing for their Children's Day worship celebration. Across the street from the Sixteenth Street Baptist Church is Kelly Ingram Park, where many of the protest marches in the city of Birmingham began, and which became notorious for the atrocious and brutal acts of Police Commissioner Eugene "Bull" Connor and the Birmingham police as they turned dogs and fire hoses on black children of Birmingham.

In Selma, we walked across the Edmund Pettus Bridge, which was the site of "Bloody Sunday" on March 7, 1965 - when hundreds of blacks and some whites gathered in an effort to march across the bridge towards Montgomery to demand voting rights, only to be violently tear-gassed, cattle-prodded, bloodily beaten and turned back by state and local authorities. In Selma, we also visited Brown Chapel African Methodist Episcopal Church, the place where over 600 persons gathered to sing, pray, strategize and receive marching orders in their ongoing efforts to take the 54 mile journey from Selma to Montgomery.

At the conclusion of both of these doctoral immersions in Alabama, I was struck by how far we as a society have come, and yet how far we have to go. There was a real sense of hope – and the presence of God in our small, diverse groups - as together we chose to be the church – *Beloved Community* - with one another. We realized that it would not have been possible 40 years prior for 20 ministers from diverse backgrounds to travel in relative peace and safety throughout Alabama. Furthermore, we realized that all of us – women, men, black, white, Asian, Native American and Latino/a - either had, or were likely to attain a doctoral degree from a major mainline theological school, and that this would not have been a realistic prospect 40 years ago.

We also recognized that there was hope for the church and society in the fact that largely because of the heroic efforts of persons in places like Montgomery, Birmingham and Selma - the Civil Rights Act was passed by Congress in 1964, and the Voting Rights Act was enacted in 1965, signed into law by a U.S. president who was a son of the American South, Lyndon B. Johnson.

As a society, we have made some progress in that we don't hear or read of as many overt and violent acts of racism as we did in the 1950s and 60s. The rights of African Americans, Hispanics, Native Americans, Asians, and other ethnic minorities, along with the rights of women and other historically marginalized persons have been enhanced in some ways.

And yet, churches in America continue to be largely segregated. It is interesting to note that each of the aforementioned Alabama congregations, Dexter Avenue, Sixteenth Street, and Brown Chapel are probably as racially segregated today was they were in the 1960's. They are not alone - as First Baptist and First United Methodist Churches in Birmingham – two of the prominent congregations addressed by Dr. Martin Luther King, Jr. in his Letter from the Birmingham Jail in 1963 - are among the many predominantly white congregations that also remain as racially segregated today as they were 40 years ago.

Despite some hopeful signs, I left Alabama each time wondering how far the church has really come, and how far we have to go to become the *Beloved Community* that Christ calls us to be. This is the *"Problem of Sunday Morning."*

In conclusion, though segregation indeed continues to abound in many churches (as it does in many other sectors of society), I believe there is hope. Charles Marsh wrote in *The Beloved Community: How Faith Shapes Social Justice, from the Civil Rights Movement to Today,* "Eleven o'clock Sunday may be the most segregated hour of the week as far as any particular parish goes, but it is the most integrated hour of the week as far as the kingdom goes. (Marsh, 215) Once again Marsh writes:

> The hope that we must nurture is the hope that all will be made whole in the history of redemption and

> that together we will join hands and learn to live in the sobering light of God's promise. (Marsh, 212)

Despite the persistent "problem of Sunday morning" we must not lose hope. My hope is rooted in the possibilities that we will continue to discover ways to capitalize on those experiences and encounters that will lead to us being intentional, inclusive community. This is the hope that must be realized if we are to be the church – the *Beloved Community* - that Christ calls us to become, and this is the hope that we must attain to if "the problem of Sunday morning" is to ever be expunged from our existential reality.

-11-

LESSONS FOR LIVING

(This sermon was preached at Lovely Lane United Methodist Church, Baltimore, Maryland in March 2011.)

"Therefore, if you are offering your gift at the altar and there remember that your brother or sister has something against you, leave your gift there in front of the altar. First go and be reconciled to them; then come and offer your gift." (Matthew 5:23-24; 21-37)

In chapters 5-7 of the Gospel of Matthew, we find what has come to be known as the Sermon on the Mount. Most scholars believe that these teachings of Jesus – rather than being a single sermon shared by the Lord at one particular time – is a series of sayings and teachings of Jesus offered over a period of time – and are compiled here by the gospel writer, Matthew. We find a similar series of teachings in the Gospel of Luke – that have come to be known as the Sermon on the Plain (Luke 6:17-49).

In these teachings, Jesus offers insight on various issues affecting the lives of the people of his day. In many ways, these are ethical teachings – relating to right ways of living – and the ways that those who would be God-followers – Christians – should treat one another. These are lessons for living as Christian disciples – followers of Jesus Christ.

In the 1930's, German theologian Dietrich Bonhoeffer wrote his seminal book – *The Cost of Discipleship* in which he offered commentary on the Sermon on the Mount. Essentially, Bonhoeffer's assessment of the Sermon on the Mount, and the teachings of Jesus is that these are a caution against what he referred to as cheap forms of grace, and that it is through our Christian discipleship that God makes significant claims on how we are to live our lives. In other words, it will cost each of us some things if we choose to follow Jesus.

In the section of the Sermon on the Mount that is a part of the lectionary readings for the day (Matt. 5:21-37), we find teachings that deal with what are apparently four unrelated matters of anger, adultery, divorce and oaths. With Jesus's teaching on these four issues, we find lessons as to how we are to relate with each other – lessons as to the implications of our actions and inactions on others.

Perhaps one of the most radical aspects of Jesus' extension of the law here is his internalization of it, so that not only our behaviors (how we outwardly treat each other), but our attitudes and emotions fall within the scope of God's concern for us. Of course, this is not new within the context of Jewish thinking. Throughout Hebrew Scriptures, the law is to be taken to heart and not only to be outwardly observed.

Jesus redirects the thoughts of his listeners from outward acts to internal orientation - from murder to anger, and from adultery to lust. It is one thing to behave rightly. It is another thing for our hearts to be oriented toward love. It is one thing to recite creeds, and yet another thing to live out deeds. Just as it is easier to make a sacrifice at the temple than it is to do justice (Micah 6), so it is easier to keep the commandment against murder than it is to avoid anger in one's heart, which might be that which leads to physical harm. Indeed, it could often be easier to give an offering to God who we cannot see, than to forgive our neighbor who we can see.

In the aftermath of the assassination attempt on Congresswoman Gabrielle Giffords – and the death of six persons in January of this year in Tuscan, Arizona – much of the public discourse that has followed has centered on the lack of civility in our society today – and the ways that people talk to one another and treat one another – and how the heightened levels of incivility in our words may impact increased levels of physical violence across society.

A few days after the violent attacks in Arizona, at the President's State of the Union address, Republicans and Democrats chose to share in a symbolic act of civility as they sat side-by-side with each other rather than sitting across the political aisle, as is customarily the case. The challenge is for this symbolic act of civility to become real in ways that help those charged with leading the nation and governing on both sides of the political aisle to move beyond partisan politics and to discover ways of collaboration for the greater good.

The teachings of Jesus are lessons for living. These lessons should lead each of us who have offered our lives as disciples of Jesus Christ to pause and think about how we treat our neighbors and even how we treat those who may be our enemies. For in another section of the Sermon on the Mount – Jesus says that we are to love even our enemies.

The good news of Epiphany is that God is present for us in Christ. Jesus, the light of the world, is re-ordering the relationships of the world, and reorienting our lives in ways that point us to God and toward loving each other. God in Christ points us persistently toward reconciliation and restoration. God in Christ is incarnate among us guiding our outward actions and our inward attitudes. Thanks be to God.

-12-

A PRAYER FOR OUR CHILDREN (2015)

This past January and August, I was privileged to go on another two pilgrimages to Alabama to study and retrace some of the steps of the American Civil Rights movement. On those pilgrimages, we visited various places in the cities of Montgomery, Birmingham and Selma. I am finally at a point where I can reflect on the impact of these two trips.

Something that struck me differently this time is the profound level of violence perpetrated against children during the movement. The cases of the deaths of Emmett Till in Money, Mississippi on August 28, 1955, and the four girls murdered during the bombing of Sixteenth Street Baptist Church in Birmingham on September 15, 1963 are well documented. While walking through Kelly Ingram Park in Birmingham, I was struck by the violence and brutality perpetrated by Police Commissioner Eugene "Bull" Connor and many other police officers in Birmingham against the children of the city on numerous occasions.

Today, we pray for the safety of all children of the world, and we pray especially for those families whose children have been victimized by violence, and who may otherwise bear the undue burdens of want and need. Amen.

-13-

DREAM - VISIONS OF BELOVED COMMUNITY

(This lecture was delivered at the "Facing the Future" Conference, sponsored by the General Commission on Religion and Race of the United Methodist Church in Los Angeles, CA. in May 2011.)

As we gather to reflect upon what it means to dream, perhaps it is most fitting that we recall that in our nation's capital almost 48 years ago, Rev. Dr. Martin Luther King, Jr. shared his dream and what he envisioned for our world. We recall that Dr. King dreamt of a world where the descendants of former slaves and former slave-owners would someday be able to sit down together at the table of sisterhood and brotherhood… a world where little children would someday live in a nation where they would not be judged by the color of their skin, but by the content of their character.

Dr. King dreamt a world where we would all grow to see the face of God in Native Americans and Hispanics, Whites and Asians, Blacks, Jews, Muslims, Buddhists, Hindus, and persons from all other racial, ethnic, social, cultural and religious backgrounds.

In his seminal poem "I Dream a World!" Langston Hughes shared:

I dream a world where no man
No other man will scorn,
Where love will bless the earth
And peace its path adorn.
I dream a world where all
Will know sweet freedom's way,
Where greed no longer saps the soul
Nor avarice blights the day.
A world I dream where black or white,
Whatever race you be,
Will share the bounties of the earth
And every man is free,
Where wretchedness will hang its head
And Joy, like pearl,
Attends the needs of all mankind-
Of such I dream my world!

The theological basis of Dr. King's dream was a singular vision of the realization of *Beloved Community.* This vision was rooted in the biblical notion of *agape* (God's unconditional love), and was the ultimate goal for society. (see Smith and Zepp, 1974, 129-153)

King asserted that "all life is interrelated." One of his fundamental beliefs was in the kinship of all persons. He believed all life is part of a single process; all living things are interrelated; and all persons are sisters and brothers. All have a place in the *Beloved Community*.

Beloved Community and Hope

King's conception of *Beloved Community* was intricately connected with the notion of hope. For King, Christian hope essentially served as another foundation for his vision of *Beloved Community.* In one of his later sermons, "The Meaning of Hope," he defined hope as that quality which is "necessary for life." (Baker-Fletcher, 132)

He asserted that hope was to be viewed as "animated and undergirded by faith and love." In his mind, if you had hope, you had faith in something. "Hope is generated and animated by love, and is undergirded by faith." Thus, hope shares the belief that "all reality hinges on moral foundations." (Baker-Fletcher)

In King's view, hope had a transformative quality that keeps human beings "alive" both spiritually and psychologically. (Baker-Fletcher) Hope, therefore, is "one of the basic structures of an adequate life." And so it was that King would share in the "I Have a Dream" speech his belief that "with this faith, we will be able to hew out of the mountain of despair, a stone of hope." This leads us to several questions:

- Where do you see glimmers of hope for the church and society today?
- Where are we called to dare to dream?
- Where and what are our dreams and visions today?

Holding onto Hope

With the fragmentation of our days, we are yet afforded great opportunities to heed the words of the prophet Joel to "dream dreams and see visions" of a better future for our churches and society.

King dared to dream and envision:

- A world of peace and love among all women and men, girls and boys…
- A world where we would study war no more…
- A world where poverty, hunger and homelessness would be eradicated…
- A world where violence and abuse would exist no longer.

There's the story of an eagle. As it was nested and born, the eagle by chance found itself growing up among a group of prairie chickens. As the eagle grew older, it learned to live like a prairie chicken; it ate like a prairie chicken; it moved like a prairie chicken; it even started to quack like a prairie chicken. And it never learned to fly.

As it continued to mature, the eagle realized that there was something that made it different from the prairie chickens that it had grown up with. Unlike the prairie chickens, the eagle's wings began to expand, and it had the urge to fly.

One day, the eagle's owner realized that the eagle was about to fly off, and decided to clip the eagle's wings so that it could not fly. And so the eagle never realized that it was an eagle and might have the ability to fly, and thus continued to live as a prairie chicken for the rest of its life.

Too many of us continue to see ourselves as (and act like) prairie chickens. Too many people never come to realize that they can fly like an eagle.

In another of his poems, Langston Hughes encourages us:

> Hold fast to dreams
> For if dreams die
> Life is a broken-winged bird
> That cannot fly.
> Hold fast to dreams
> For when dreams go
> Life is a barren field
> Frozen with snow.

Where's hope? Hope can be found in the possibilities that we will continue to discover ways to capitalize on those experiences and encounters that will lead to us being intentional and inclusive community. This is the hope that must be realized if we are to be the – the *Beloved Community* that Dr. King imagined.

In the days ahead, may we continue to conjure the audacity to dream dreams and see visions. May we have the temerity to hope against all that seems to rise against hope, and may we have the courage and tenacity to forever hold onto hope.

-14-

THERE'S HOPE

(This sermon was preached at Epworth Chapel United Methodist Church, Baltimore, MD in December 8, 2013.)

At that time Mary got ready and hurried to a town in the hill country of Judea, where she entered Zechariah's home and greeted Elizabeth. When Elizabeth heard Mary's greeting, the baby leaped in her womb, and Elizabeth was filled with the Holy Spirit. In a loud voice she exclaimed: "Blessed are you among women, and blessed is the child you will bear! But why am I so favored, that the mother of my Lord should come to me? As soon as the sound of your greeting reached my ears, the baby in my womb leaped for joy. Blessed is she who has believed that the Lord would fulfill his promises to her!" (Luke 1:39-45)

In this day and age, there seems to be a paucity of hope among us, and thus we are led to wonder what is there about which we can really be hopeful. An analysis and inventory of our world, and the days of our lives would indicate that we teeter (and teeter) on the brink of hopelessness and despair.

The news abounds with such signs. The Affordable Care Act (what is also known as Obamacare) has been consistently threatened with failure and demise over the past several weeks. Sequestration, fiscal cliffs, foreclosure, shutdowns, bankruptcy have become a part of our everyday vernacular and reality.

Crime continues to infect too many of our neighborhoods. In Baltimore city, again it is projected that there will be over 200 people murdered by the end of 2013. Global conflict and wars persist, natural disasters kill thousands around the world, preventable diseases like AIDS and malaria continue to afflict too many of our sisters and brothers – especially in the two-thirds world. The days of our lives often appear to be hopeless – don't they?

And yet, the death of Nelson Mandela (three days ago) should remind us that regardless of how hopeless things might appear, regardless of how dire our circumstances may seem, regardless of the despair and disappointment that we face, there's always some reason to hope, and we should never stop hoping.

History shows that South African Apartheid brought on some of the most despicable forms of human atrocity and suffering in modern history. We should not forget that through decades, the majority population in South Africa and in other southern African countries like Rhodesian (Zimbabwe) and Mozambique were subjected to deplorable living conditions under oppressive political and military power structures. And it was people like Nelson Mandela – even in the midst of 27 years of imprisonment – who never stopped hoping that the day would come that Apartheid would come to an end, and that all people – blacks and whites - would have rights to live freely as they were created by God.

And we know that the apparent paucity of hope that I began this message talking about is not new or exclusive to the present age. Luke tells us that as the angel Gabriel came to Mary to announce that she was about to give birth to God's son, Israel - faced similar apparent hopelessness.

In that day, God's people found themselves under Roman occupation. Their land had been overtaken by political and economic structures that served to oppress them and subject them to human suffering not unlike Apartheid in South Africa, slavery in America, imperialism in India, the Holocaust in Germany or ethnic cleansing in Africa and Europe.

In the midst of all of this, the Israelites had been waiting for 700 years for the coming of the promised Savior – the Messiah - into the world. They had been waiting for the words of the prophet Isaiah to come to pass, that *"unto us a Child is born, unto us a Son will be given."* (Isaiah 9:7) They had been waiting, and in the midst of it, some 700 years later, they still found themselves wondering whether God's promise of a Savior would ever come to pass for them.

And God sent an angel to Mary to offer some words of hope to her and to the world that things were about to change and that hope was about to enter into their world.

There's hope! One of the things I've learned about hope is that there are times when we tend to trivialize and even mythologize hope to the point that we often don't recognize it when it is in our midst. I say this to suggest that if we take time to look around, we will see hope all around us.

Children laughing and playing - that's hope. Music in our ears - that's hope. Food on our tables, clothes on our backs, shoes on our feet, new awakenings - that's hope. Opportunities afforded and doors opened – that's hope. Jeremiah said it best when he sang, *"morning by morning new mercies I see..."* (Lamentation 3:23) - that's hope.

Hope is real, and should be real to you and me. Hope is what German theologian Jürgen Moltmann wrote about when he wrote – "Hope alone is to be called "realistic" because it alone takes seriously the possibilities with which all reality is fraught. Hope does not take things as they happen to stand or to lie, but as progressing, moving things with possibilities of change." (Moltmann, 25)

Hope is real, and should be real to you and me. The hope that Moltmann wrote about is the same hope that contemporary neo-soul singer India Arie sings about –

> Every time I turn on the T.V. (There's Hope)
> Somebody's acting crazy (There's Hope)
> If you let it, it will drive you crazy (There's Hope)
> but I'm takin' back my power today (There's Hope)
> Gas prices they just keep on rising (There's Hope)
> The government they keep on lying
> but we gotta keep on surviving
> Keep living our truth and do the best we can do.
> (There's Hope)

Hope is real, and should be real to you and me. The hope that Moltmann writes about and Arie sings about is the very same hope that we sing about in the church –

My hope is built on nothing less
than Jesus's blood and righteousness.
I dare not trust the sweetest frame,
but wholly lean on Jesus name…
("My Hope is Built")

There's Hope!

-15-

THE POWER OF LOVE: MOHANDAS GANDHI AND NONVIOLENCE FOR THE 21ST CENTURY

(This lecture was delivered at St. Mary's Seminary and University, Baltimore, Maryland on February 10, 2012.)

Mohandas K. Gandhi was one of the few persons in modern history to lead in the struggle for human progress simultaneously on moral, religious, political and cultural fronts. His life and praxis of nonviolence impacted many persons in India and across the world in the promotion of peace and love with justice, and continues to impact persons, institutions and governments today.

With the ongoing proliferation today of violence, war, local and global conflict, terrorism and geopolitical discord, Gandhi's philosophy and praxis can be helpful in the discovery of non-violent approaches to peacemaking, community-building, conflict resolution and social transformation in the 21st century.

Huston Smith, in *The World's Religions* offers that "the face of Hinduism for the West is Mohandas Gandhi." According to Smith, "Most responsible for awakening the West to the realities of the East (and the beauty of Hinduism) was a little man who weighed not much more than a hundred pounds and whose possessions when he died totaled two dollars. (Huston Smith, 1991, 13) If his picture were to appear on this page it would be recognized immediately. How many other portraits would be recognized universally? Someone ventured a few years ago that there were only three: those of Charlie Chaplin, Mickey Mouse, and Mahatma Gandhi – "whose essence of being is great" as the title "mahatma" would be literally translated. (Huston Smith)

The achievement for which the world credited Gandhi was the peaceful British withdrawal from India. What is not as well-known is that among his own people, he lowered a barrier thought by many to be much more formidable than that of British colonialism in India, racism in the United States or Apartheid in South Africa - renaming and redefining "untouchables" in India as "harijan", God's children, and raising them to human status.

Mohandas Gandhi was born in India in 1869 into the Vaishya caste (merchants, farmers, and craftspeople). (see Thomas Merton, 1964) His father, however, was involved in law and politics. His mother was a very religious person. A devout Hindu, she engaged in self-discipline, purification and other religious observances. Gandhi's India was dominated by British colonialism. In his hometown of Rajkot, he experienced early segregation. The British reserved for themselves the best part of town; Indians were restricted to the slums. At school, he was taught in English, under the assumption that everything Indian was inferior. Gandhi disliked this arrangement. He felt that Indians needed the pride of language, custom and history. With his pride of self and people, Gandhi studied both Sanskrit and Persian. (Merton)

When he decided to go to England to study law, Gandhi confronted the stark reality of the caste system. This led him to declare war against the strictures and harshness of the caste system, and this conviction remained with him for the rest of his life.

In England, Gandhi's philosophy of nonviolence began to take shape. He studied the ideas of Hindus, Buddhists and Christians. He was moved as well by the writings of American authors such as Ralph Waldo Emerson and Henry David Thoreau. Thoreau's ideas, especially on civil disobedience, impressed Gandhi. His encounter with the New Testament, especially with Jesus and the Sermon on the Mount, had a profound impact on his thinking.

The Development of Satyagraha

Faith was the center of Gandhi's life. He believed in God, and in truth. "What I want to achieve, what I have been striving and pining to achieve these thirty years," he wrote in his autobiography, "is self-realization, to see God face to face. I live and move and have my being in pursuit of this goal. All that I do by way of speaking and writing, and all my ventures in the political field, are directed to the same end." Gandhi saw the face of God in the poorest peasant and in the struggle of nonviolent resistance and love in the public realm. He sought to uncover truth at every turn and found that justice and nonviolence sprang from the journey in truth. "You may be sent to the gallows, or put to torture, but if you have truth in you, you will experience an inner joy." Truth, for Gandhi, was the essence of life. (John Dear, 1988)

As someone whose entire adult life was consumed with fighting against such injustices as racial discrimination in South Africa, British rule in India, and ugly social practices within his own society, Gandhi sought to develop an approach of how moral persons could and should act in such struggles. He found both the methods of rational discussion and violence – the traditional methods which appealed to people in addressing injustice – as unsatisfactory to various degrees, and thus sought to discover an alternative and more powerful method.

Gandhi was particularly disturbed by the ease with which violence had been rationalized and used throughout history. He appreciated that violence was born out of frustration, and many who used it resorted to it only because they saw no other way to fight entrenched injustices, and that much of the blame for its use had to be laid at the doorsteps of a morally blind and narrow-minded dominant group.

Gandhi opposed violence on both ontological and moral grounds. From an ontological perspective, violence denied the fact that all human beings had souls, and that they were capable of appreciating and pursuing good. Furthermore, in order to be justified in taking the extreme step of harming or killing someone, one had to assume that one was absolutely right, and the opponent totally wrong, and that violence would definitely achieve the desired result.

On moral grounds, every successful act of violence encouraged the belief that it was the only effective way to achieve the desired goal, and developed the habit of turning to violence every time one ran into opposition. Society thus turned to violence, and it never felt compelled to explore alternatives. Violence also tended to generate an inflationary spiral. Every successful use of violence blunted the community's moral sensibility and raised its threshold of violence, so that over time, an increasingly larger amount of violence became necessary to achieve the same results. In Gandhi's view the facts that almost every revolution in history has led to terror, devoured its children, and failed to create a better society were proof that the traditional theory of revolution was fatally flawed.

Gandhi concluded that since the two methods (rational discussion and violence) of fighting against injustice were inadequate and deeply flawed, a third method was necessary. It should activate the soul, mobilize individuals' latent moral energies, appeal to both the head and heart, and create a climate conducive to peaceful resolution of conflict conducted in a spirit of mutual good will.

The formative ideas of Gandhi's philosophy began to take shape in the years he worked to better the social and economic conditions of Indians in South Africa. Gandhi spent 20 years of his life in South Africa as an acknowledged leader of the Indian people. (J. Deotis Roberts, 2000, 36) Rajmohan Gandhi, research professor at the Center of Policy Research, New Delhi, India has suggested that much of

Gandhi's view on nonviolence can be traced to his personal experiences and early encounters with bigotry on his journey to South Africa in 1893. (Rajmohan Gandhi, 1995) Rajmohan Gandhi offers an account, depicted in the Attenborough film, of the well-known incident when Mohandas Gandhi was ejected from the railway train at the station of Pietermaritzburg in the year 1893:

> The barrister trained in London, he was holding a first-class ticket and had just arrived in South Africa – he had been there hardly a week. Because he did not have the right skin color and did not move to the van compartment when asked, he was thrown out. Then he made a journey by train, coach, and train again, eventually arriving, via Johannesburg in Pretoria. Along the way he was roughly beaten on the coach because he refused to sit as ordered on the floor. He tried to spend the stopover night in Johannesburg in a hotel, but was told that there was no room. He had experiences that were not very pleasant. On a Sunday evening he arrived in Pretoria, his destination. Not sure of what lay ahead of him, and remembering that he could not get accommodations in Johannesburg, he wondered where he would spend his first night in Pretoria. He decided to consult the man who was checking tickets at the exit for ideas. While he was having this conversation, a Black American noticed the predicament of the young man from India (Gandhi was only 23 at this time), went up to Gandhi, and asked the young man if he could help. (R. Gandhi)

> Mohandas Gandhi explained his anxiety. The African American said, "I have an American friend, Mr. Johnston, who has a hotel in Pretoria. He might put you up." So they walked from the station to the hotel, this man whose name is not known and Gandhi. Gandhi describes the incident in his autobiography, written 33 years later, but does not give the name of the Good Samaritan. At the hotel the man introduced Gandhi to Mr. Johnston, who said: "You can stay in the hotel if you are willing to eat in your room. If I took you to the dining room, the other guests might not like it." Gandhi hated conditions of this sort but he made the compromise. "All right," he said. A little later there was a knock on the door, and Gandhi thought it was a man with a tray. But it was Mr. Johnston himself, who said: "I have spoken to the other guests in the hotel and they are willing for you to eat in the dining room." As far as I know it was Gandhi's first encounter with Americans, one Black and the other White. (R. Gandhi)

Rajmohan Gandhi points out that it remains an interesting fact of history that the man who enabled Gandhi to have a roof and a bed in Pretoria was an African American. As is evident from a sketch of Mohandas Gandhi's early life, he was "born to rebel." His philosophy would inevitably be a philosophy for action. It was to be more than a philosophy for social engagement; it was to become a philosophy for social transformation. He came to believe that every person was of infinite worth, equal value, and that oppressed people should struggle for their equality. According to Gandhi, they must fight peacefully and they must not hurt others while doing so. He strongly believed that unjust laws should not be obeyed, but that people should not be violent in their attempt to change the law.

In 1907, Gandhi, who was still in South Africa, again read Henry David Thoreau. In seeking to conceptualize his philosophy, Gandhi borrowed the anglicized term "civil disobedience" from Thoreau, which was more often referred to as "passive resistance." But Gandhi was not satisfied with either. Both were too narrowly conceived; they appeared to be negative, passive and weak. They could easily denigrate into hatred and would likely opt, finally, for violence. Thus, civil disobedience and passive resistance became obsolete for Gandhi.

In a magazine called *Indian Opinion,* which he edited for a time in South Africa, Gandhi offered a small prize to be "awarded to the reader who invented the best designation for our struggle." One of his cousins, Maganlal Gandhi, produced a word that seemed almost right, *sadagraha,* which means "firmness in a good cause." Mohandas Gandhi corrected it to *Satyagraha... Satya* means "Truth"; *graha* means "firmness, tenacity, holding on." (William H. Shannon, 154)

"I thus began," Gandhi says, "to call the Indian movement *Satyagraha,* that is to say the Force that is born in truth and love, or nonviolence," and gave up the use of the phrase "passive resistance." On other occasions, Gandhi called it "Soul Force," "Love Force," or "Truth Force." *Sat* in *Satyagraha* means "being," "that which is," "truth." For Gandhi, *Sat* was "the only correct and fully significant name for God. (Shannon, 153)

The conception of S*atyagraha* became fundamental to Gandhi's life and activity. (see Merton) It is "truth-taking" or "the taking of vows of truthfulness." Its root and meaning is "holding on to truth" and, by extension, resistance to evil by nonviolent means. This "truth force" is possible because it excludes the use of violence, because humans are capable of grasping the truth (but not in an absolute sense) and are not competent to punish. Theologically, truth in an absolute sense is God or Ultimate Being.

A concept that was closely related to *Satyagraha* and used by Gandhi in the discussion of the meaning of nonviolent action was the principle of *ahimsa* (non-injury). This term is borrowed from the Jains. Jainism, founded by Mahavira, is one of the oldest personally founded religions in India. The Jains were known for their doctrine of the non-injury of all forms of life. It was this religious concept of *ahimsa* that attracted Gandhi. Historically, Jains became merchants rather than farmers because they did not wish to destroy any form of (sentient) life. Even today, Jaina women wear veils over their noses and mouths to avoid breathing in any form of insect life. (Roberts, 37)

For Gandhi, *ahimsa* was the basic law of being. It can be used as the most effective principle for social action since it is ingrained deeply in human nature and corresponds to humanity's innate desire for peace, justice, freedom and personal dignity. *Himsa* (violence or injury) is just the opposite – it degrades, corrupts and destroys. It feeds on the tendency to meet force with force, hatred with hatred. This plan of action leads to progressive denigration. Nonviolence, on the other hand, heals and restores humanity's best nature, while providing the best means of restoring a social order of justice and freedom. *Ahimsa* is not preoccupied with the seizure of power as an end in itself; it is a way of transforming relationships in order to bring about a peaceful transfer of power. (Roberts)

Gandhi's conception of nonviolence - *Satyagraha* - began with the spiritual disciplines of prayer, solitude and fasting. By avoiding power in all its forms of violence and control, and by renouncing the desire for immediate results, Gandhi discovered that one could be reduced to zero. From this ground zero of emptiness, the compassionate love of God - nonviolence – could grow. At this point, Gandhi wrote, the individual becomes "irresistible" and one's nonviolence becomes "all-pervasive." Nonviolence, the power of the powerless, Gandhi believed, is the power of God, the power of truth and love that goes beyond the physical world into the realm of the spiritual. This power can overcome death, as God revealed through the nonviolence of Jesus, his crucifixion, and subsequent resurrection in the resisting community. (Dear)

Gandhi's experiments in Truth revealed that the mandate of the Sermon on the Mount – to love one's enemies – is of critical importance. In all of Gandhi's public uses of nonviolence, he always manifested a desire for reconciliation and friendship with his opponent.

Gandhi was not only interested in ousting the British from control of the Indian continent; he wanted to end the ancient and oppressive caste system among his own people. He always tried to stand with the outcasts of society and to speak up for the rights of the marginalized. In India, such solidarity primarily meant taking the radical and scandalizing public stand on behalf of the so-called untouchables. Gandhi, instead, called them *harigans,* or "children of God," and begged his fellow Indians to banish untouchability from their hearts and lives. (Dear)

The ancient Hindu *Laws of Manu* required devotees to live according to a stratified caste system, one that persists in India today, despite efforts by Gandhi and his followers to reform it. "For the sake of the preservation of this entire creation," we are told, *Brahman*, the Supreme Being, "assigned separate duties to the classes which had sprung from his mouth, arms, thighs, and feet." (Fisher and Bailey 2000, 70) Humans who are born as *brahmans* have the duty of "teaching, studying, performing sacrificial rites," making others perform such rites, "and giving away and receiving gifts." The code lists the other three castes: The *kshatriya* who are warriors, political leaders and vassals; the *vaishya* who are farmers and merchants, and the *shudra*, who are servants of the other three classes. Mary Pat Fisher explains that a fifth group not mentioned in the excerpt of the *Law of Manu* were "untouchables", those who were effectively "outcasts". Despite their marginalized status, the code required charitable giving which "provided a safety net for those at the bottom of this hierarchical system." (Fisher and Bailey, 97) This is the group that Gandhi preferred to call the "*harijan*" or "children of God."

For Gandhi, *Satyagraha* essentially aimed to penetrate the barriers of prejudice, ill-will, dogmatism, self-righteousness and selfishness, and to reach out to and activate the soul of the opponent. However degenerate, dogmatic or violent an individual might be, according to the Satyagrahi, he had a soul, and hence the capacity to feel for other human beings and, on some level, acknowledge their common humanity. *Satyagraha* was in essence, "surgery of the soul," a way of activating "soul force" for Gandhi, and "suffering love" was the best way to accomplish this. As he put it:

> I have come to this fundamental conclusion that if you want something really important to be done, you must not merely satisfy the reason, you must move the heart also. The appeal of reason is more to the head, but the penetration of the heart comes from suffering. It opens up the inner understanding in man. Suffering is the badge of the human race, not the sword.

Gandhi explained the effectiveness of *Satyagraha* in terms of the spiritual impact of suffering love. The Satyagrahi's love of his opponent served to disarm the opponent, defused his feelings of anger and hatred, and mobilized his higher nature. And his uncomplaining suffering denied his opponent the pleasure of victory.

In light of this, Gandhi shared that India should work to overcome what he termed the Seven Deadly Social Sins: (1) Politics without principle; (2) Wealth without work; (3) Commerce without morality; (4) Pleasure without conscience; (5) Education without character; (6) Science without humanity; and (7) Worship without sacrifice.

He came to believe that every person is of equal value, and that oppressed people should struggle for their equality. Gandhi's philosophy was inevitably a philosophy for action. He stated that "A nonviolent revolution is not a program of seizure of power. It is a program of transformation of relationships, ending in peaceful transfer of power."

Satyagraha and the Christian Love-ethic

Mohandas Gandhi provided a deep reservoir of ideas from which many peacemakers of the twentieth century drew, and from which those of the 21st century might draw, as well. For instance, Howard Thurman, Martin Luther King, Jr., and many others believed that they were better equipped with the most rigorous understanding of nonviolent principles due to their exposure to the thought and praxis of Gandhi. Their respective exposure served to clarify and codify their thinking with regard to nonviolence, while also serving as an impetus for their ongoing search for peaceful community.

Many African-American leaders had gone to India beginning in the 1930s to seek Gandhi's advice and to study his nonviolent method. The American Civil Rights movement of the 1950s and 1960s confirmed Gandhi's hope. Embarking on "a serious intellectual quest for a method to eliminate social evil," Martin Luther King, Jr. had turned to a number of writers including Karl Marx, and found them unhelpful. An address by Mordecai Johnson, then the President of Howard University, alerted King to the importance of Gandhi's teachings and the potential value of *Satyagraha.*

In the Montgomery, Alabama bus boycott and protests of 1955-56, King saw the connection with Gandhi's nonviolence. "I had come to see early that the Christian doctrine of love operating through the Gandhian method of nonviolence was one of the most potent weapons available to the Negro in his struggle for freedom." (Martin Luther King, Jr., *1958,* 71) King said that a white woman who sympathized with the protest movement wrote a letter to the editor that was published in the *Montgomery Advertiser* comparing the bus protest with Gandhi's movement in India. Before long, people were talking about Gandhi in Montgomery. "People who had never heard of the little brown saint of India were now saying his name with an air of familiarity," King wrote. (King 1958)

Gandhi's concept of *Satyagraha,* or truth-force, was understood almost immediately as "love-force" by Martin Luther King, Jr. at the apex of the American Civil Rights movement. King saw a direct connection between Truth and

Love, and like Gandhi, essentially equated the two. He saw in Gandhi the means by which the love-ethic in the teachings of Jesus – especially in the Sermon on the Mount - could become effective for social transformation. King also saw that it was not necessary to limit the Christian love-ethic to individual relationships; the love-ethic could be applied to conflicts between races, cultures, tribes and nations.

In a very clear way, King stated his discovery: "Gandhi gave me the Method and Jesus gave me the Message."

King pointed out his particular attraction to Gandhi's notion of the love-ethic:

> As I read I became fascinated by (Gandhi's) campaigns of nonviolent resistance.... The whole concept of Satyagraha...was profoundly significant to me. As I delved deeper into the philosophy of Gandhi, my skepticism concerning the power of love gradually diminished, and I came to see for the first time its potency in the area of social reform. Prior to reading Gandhi, I had about concluded that the ethics of Jesus were only effective in individual relationships.... But after reading Gandhi, I saw how utterly mistaken I was.

Gandhi was probably the first person in history to lift the love-ethic of Jesus above a mere interaction between individuals to a powerful and effective social force on a larger scale. Love, for Gandhi, was a potent instrument for social and collective

> transformation. It was in this Gandhian emphasis on love and nonviolence that I discovered the method for social reform that I had been seeking for so many months. The intellectual and moral satisfaction that I failed to gain from the utilitarianism of Bentham and Mill, the revolutionary methods of Marx and Lenin, the social contracts theory of Hobbes, the "back to nature" optimism of Rousseau, and the superman philosophy of Nietzsche, I found in the nonviolent resistance philosophy of Gandhi. I came to feel that this was the only morally and practically sound method open to oppressed people in their struggle for freedom. (King, "Pilgrimage to Nonviolence in Washington 1986, 35)

In his reflections on the significance of Gandhi within the context of Christianity, King wrote:

> It is ironic, yet inescapably true that the greatest Christian of the modern world was a man who never embraced Christianity… I believe that in some marvelous way, God worked through Gandhi, and the spirit of Jesus Christ saturated his life. (King,1958, 85-97)

King felt that Gandhi was probably the first person in history to lift the love-ethic of Jesus Christ to a place where it could become an effective instrument for collective transformation. Thus, the method of social reform, which had eluded King and others in the quest for racial justice in

America, was now found in the way that Gandhi understood and appropriated truth (as love).

Howard Thurman was another leading American Christian religious figure who was attracted to the thinking and praxis of Mohandas Gandhi. Thurman was extremely impressed with Gandhi's ideas on the power of nonviolence as a method which positively responds to the spiritual needs of humanity, while at the same time accomplishing the necessary political transformation of the social order. (Yates 1964, 104-109) Certainly, Gandhi's success in India was solid evidence for nonviolence. Gandhi reinforced, confirmed and provided deeper insights about the efficacy of nonviolence for Thurman.

In 1936, Howard Thurman and his wife, Sue Bailey Thurman, along with Rev. and Ms. Edward Carroll journeyed to India to visit with Gandhi. On that visit, Thurman asked Gandhi to define nonviolence. Gandhi said he hoped it would be love in the Pauline sense, love as spelled out in the letter to the Corinthians, plus the struggle for justice. Gandhi asked his American visitors if they would sing a Negro spiritual for him. Gandhi was greatly moved as Mrs. Thurman sang two Negro spirituals: "Were You There When They Crucified My Lord?" and "We Are Climbing Jacob's Ladder." (Roberts, 32)

After hearing these spirituals, Gandhi said to the four: "Well if it comes true it may be through the Negroes (in America) that the unadulterated message of nonviolence will be delivered to the world." (Mohandas Gandhi 1942, 124)

The end result of the conversation was that Thurman felt assured that nonviolence, as expressed in Gandhian principles, could transform whatever difficulties it confronted. The techniques might have to be refined, individuals would need to go through radical preparation to be faithful disciples of the method, large numbers of people might suffer and die, but the moral and spiritual imperatives for nonviolence would prevail over experiences of violence. (Mohandas Gandhi, 105-106)

In formulating his response to Gandhi's critique of Christianity, Thurman began to integrate Gandhian principles of unity and nonviolent social change into his own Christian pacifism and mysticism. (Fluker and Tumber 1998, 7) Thurman returned to the United States with "an enhanced interpretation of the meaning of nonviolence." (Pollard 1992, 37) From Gandhi, "a man who (was) rooted in the basic mysticism of the [Hindu] Brahma," he learned the life-affirming concepts of *ahimsa* and S*atyagraha.* Thurman found in Gandhi a kindred mind and spirit who refused to think in terms of a disconnected Truth, God, or Ultimate reality but focused his attention on that which was pre-eminently practical and spiritual. (Pollard)

The Power of Love: Towards a Framework of Non-violence in the 21st Century

In the final analysis, Mohandas Gandhi's thought and praxis offers insight for the contemporary society with regard to appropriating a love-ethic and practicing nonviolence in at least three principle areas: *Imperative, Inspiration and Integration.*

Imperative

Mohandas Gandhi spoke to the divine and moral imperative – God's calling - that persons share in seeking to eradicate racial hatred and social disintegration, and advanced the appropriation of the love-ethic as foundational for constructively moving towards the realization of authentic community. Gandhi asserted that the divine intent is for the human family to live in community as interrelated members.

As an Indian and Hindu who was conversant in various religious traditions – including Christianity - Gandhi possessed a perspective on the divine imperative of nonviolence that had been forged on the anvil of societal oppression in various contexts. In light of this, he consistently affirmed that all humankind was bound together through a common creative Force (Truth, Love, Soul). Hence, the fundamental tenets of love, truth, forgiveness and *Satyagraha* would become the spiritual means of addressing extant forms of oppression. In a world that is still plagued with brokenness, separation, suspicion, and deadly conflicts along racial, tribal and ethnic lines, it remains the urgent calling of all persons to affirm that God has created all persons, and that we are called to exist in peaceable and just community.

Given Gandhi's affinity with the Sermon on the Mount, it is clear that he could affirm, to some degree, that the imitation of the unconditional love revealed in the life and teachings of Jesus can be helpful in the quest for community. Moving toward a deeper sense of who we are as individuals and community will enable us to live more shalom-filled lives, modeled on the life of Christ. There is the obligation to treat every person as Christ Himself, respecting the other's life as if it were one's own life or the life of Christ.

Inspiration

Throughout his life, Gandhi seemed to sense, like Jesus and persons like Martin Luther King, Jr. and Dietrich Bonhoeffer, that his teachings regarding justice, love, forgiveness, equality and peace would require significant sacrifice and ultimately get him into trouble. Yet, he remained faithful to his calling and mission, and perpetually sought to live the God-inspired message that he had been given. As a "God intoxicated man", Gandhi offered a paradigm of God-centered and God-inspired servant-leadership to society. The effectiveness of Gandhi's witness is to be viewed in light of this constant striving for and connectedness with Truth (God) and the practice of *Satyagraha*. As has been shared, faith was the center of life for Gandhi. "What I want to achieve, what I have been striving and pining to achieve these thirty years," he wrote in his autobiography, "is self-realization, to see God face to face. I live and move and have my being in pursuit of this goal. All that I do by way of speaking and writing, and all my ventures in the political field, are directed to the same end." Gandhi saw the face of God in the poorest "untouchable" in his society and in the struggle of nonviolent resistance and love in the public realm.

The development of authentic community requires the same God-connectedness. In light of this, Gandhi's encouragement and ongoing legacy is that given each person's god-giftedness, each person would be inspired to "be the change that we want to see in the world."

Integration

For Mohandas Gandhi, the promise of authentic community through overcoming injustice and oppression was at the heart of the human quest for a peaceful society. All human beings are daughters and sons of God, and sisters and brothers with one another. Society is to be an embodiment of unity within history. For this reason, society is to model and strive toward unity and peace with justice, with the knowledge that unity among human beings is possible – and community is fully evident - only if there is real justice for all people.

Community - by its very nature - is integrative. Authentic community includes persons of different races, sexes, ages, religions, cultures, viewpoints, lifestyles and stages of development - and for Gandhi, class and caste - and serves to integrate persons into a whole that is greater – more actualized, dynamic and synergized – than the sum of its parts. Forms of disintegration and disunity are, therefore, to be understood as antithetical to community and to the will of God.

Conclusion

In Mohandas Gandhi's writings, teachings and actions, *Satyagraha,* and the related concept, *ahimsa,* became manifest as techniques for action toward nonviolence, peacemaking and a love-ethic that could lead to spiritual and social transformation. These constructs were not dogmatic, and neither were they static. Rather, they were dynamic and spiritual concepts, techniques and processes for action. Amidst violence, wars, terror and various other forms of social disintegration that continue to afflict society today, *Satyagraha* and *ahimsa* can serve as means of helping humanity move toward higher goals of the common good, nonviolence, authentic community and peace with justice that beckon all persons to become involved in the quest for human betterment and fulfillment.

-16-

A PRAYER FOR THE STATE OF MARYLAND

(This prayer was delivered as the Invocation to open the Maryland State Senate session on Monday, January 14, 2013 in Annapolis, Maryland.)

Gracious, all-loving and all-wise God, in the busyness of this day, we pause to offer thanks to you. We come from various places; we come with divergent perspectives; we come with a diversity of hopes, dreams and visions. But we come acknowledging that we gather in the commonality that all persons share in you, the creator of the universe.

God, we offer thanks to you for the state of Maryland. We pray that in the days ahead, you'd bless every home and every community in this great state. Bless every school and every place where your people gather for work or leisure. Bless those persons who are older and those who are younger. We pray for peace and safety for all of us who live and move throughout this state, and we pray likewise for communities like ours across our nation and around the world.

We pray that you will bless each of us gathered here. Most importantly, we ask for your blessings and guidance upon those who serve and lead the state of Maryland in elective and appointive office. Bless them with a portion of wisdom, patience, integrity, justice and compassion. Bless each of those who serve and lead that they will be forever mindful of a collective commitment to act in ways that facilitate the betterment of each person, each home, each school, each community, and each place of business in Maryland. God, be with each of us now and forever, we pray. Amen.

-17-

MULTICULTURALISM: ARE WE THERE YET?

(This essay was published by the General Commission on Religion and Race of the United Methodist Church in March 2012.)

Are we there yet? I am convinced that to speak of multiculturalism in the church today, means to take into account the ongoing complexities of race and race relations across American society in general. As I have been invited to reflect upon and write on this important question, America finds itself in the midst of tremendous turmoil surrounding the case of the death of Trayvon Martin in Sanford, Florida on February 26, 2012. Trayvon's killing, and the fact that there has not been an arrest in the case to-date, conjures painful memories for many people of the murder of Emmett Till in Money, Mississippi in 1955, and the 1992 race riots in Los Angeles, California at the acquittal of the police officers charged in the brutal beating of Rodney King.

In the aftermath of the Los Angeles riots, Cornel West wrote the important and provocative book, *Race Matters*, in which he argued at the time that race continued to matter in America, and that we as a society needed to continue to attend to race matters. Twenty years later, it is my belief that race still matters, and we still need to attend to race matters in America, in both the church and society.

We continue to grapple with what it means to interact across cultures, and with what type of discourse and action is appropriate and necessary in the areas of immigration reform, healthcare reform, the ongoing expansion of the prison industrial complex (and concomitant disproportionate arrest and incarceration rates for young black and brown men), and ongoing economic distress that points to widening inequality and income/wealth disparities between the richer and the poorer, which all serve to disproportionately affect African-Americans, Hispanics/Latinx and Native Americans.

At the election of Barack Obama as the first non-white United States president in 2008, there seemed to be heightened hope that we were closer than ever to arriving at becoming a post-racial/post-racist society. But as is seen with the rise of Tea Party politics, burgeoning right-wing extremism, and the loudening voices of those intent on "taking back their county," we are no closer to arriving at post-racism, let alone post-racialism, today than we were before President Obama's election.

As with society in general, I sense that these are times in which the church is called to engage in serious introspection, interrogation, self-examination and soul-searching as it pertains to our theological prerogative in light of the claims that the gospel of Jesus Christ makes on us to speak truth to power with clarion voice, with regard to the wounds that racism continues to inflict on the church and society. This speaking of truth would lead us to prophetically declare - as did Jesus - that God is indeed concerned about the poor among us (Luke 4:18), and that God is for the dispossessed and the disinherited – those who have the least and who are the left out among us. After loudly and clearly speaking this truth, the church must then re-double its commitment to boldly acting out and living out what we say we believe. Here, our actions must clearly align with our words - our works and our faith must be closely aligned.

What's most interesting today is how silent many white Christians seem to be when a major-party politician running for national office feels free to state that he is not concerned about the "very poor", or when justice is at the least delayed in the killing of an unarmed 17 year-old African-American boy, Trayvon Martin in Florida. These are indicators of the work that we who are the church must continue to do if we are to ever arrive at places of meaningful discourse and constructive action as it pertains to striving towards multiculturalism, color-blindness and real inclusiveness.

-18-

THE (2012) PRESIDENTIAL ELECTION - THE DAY AFTER AND HOLDING ONTO HOPE

(This essay was written and published on my Blog in the aftermath of the 2012 Presidential Election in November 2012.)

On Monday November 12th, the day before 2012 U.S. presidential election, I saw a photo of President Barack Obama hanging in effigy outside a voting site and gas station in Raleigh, N.C. With that image in my mind and on the nation's conscience, I wrote that with whomever would win this year's presidential election, it has become very clear over the past several months that we are a nation that remains significantly divided along racial lines. We are far from being a post-racial/post-racist society. And my prayer was (and continues to be) that God would grant all of us the courage to speak out and act out to address such division.

And last night, with the re-election of President Obama as the 44th president of the United States, if anything, the president's re-election says to the world that the invisible, the poor, the 47% do indeed have a voice, and do indeed matter. It is also my prayer that God will anoint the president's leadership, and that the healing of the land will begin. (2 Chronicles 7:14)

Now the real work begins for all of us. On the president's agenda for the next four years must be job creation, providing adequate and affordable healthcare for everybody, helping and empowering the poor, children and the elderly, gender justice in the workplace and beyond, bringing our men and women home from the war in Afghanistan, and bringing true honor and meaning to President Obama's Nobel Peace Prize. And for those of us who voted for him (and for all Americans) on our agenda must be a commitment to support the president and all of our elected and appointed leaders, doing our part to move our communities forward, and praying for the president and not preying on him.

-19-

A LIVING HOPE

(This sermon was delivered on January 31, 2014 (New Year's Eve) at Epworth Chapel United Methodist Church, Baltimore, MD.)

"Blessed be [God] . . . who according to God's abundant mercy has begotten us again to a living hope." (1 Peter 1:3 (3-9))

Life is hard for everybody, but it is much harder for some of us than for others. For, some of us, it sometimes gets to the point where life seems too hard to bear.

And if the truth is told, putting our faith and trust in Christ as our Savior may seem to do little to change that. Nothing in the Bible promises us a free pass merely because we are Christ's followers. Suffering will come – even for Christians. Disappointments and despair will show up – even for Christians. Trials and tribulations will come – even for Christians.

In fact, some of our wounds may not heal and some of our deficiencies may not be corrected during our lifetime. They may even get worse.

And so what is the remedy for the wounds of life… what antidote do we, as Christians, have? This is what Peter seeks to address in his first pastoral letter. In 1 Peter, the pastor is obviously seeking to offer words of encouragement for people just like you and me.

I'm sure people in the early church were very much like us. They were people seeking to walk by faith and not by sight… they were people like you and me who were seeking to live right.

And yet in the midst of their faithfulness, they found themselves wounded by the world around them. They found themselves living with faith deformed and weakened by the waves of the restless seas of the world. They found themselves broken by evil and despair in their midst.

And Peter stops to remind them with these words: *"Blessed be [God] . . . who according to God's abundant mercy has begotten us again to a living hope." (1Peter 1:3)*

What Peter could offer the people in his faith community was the prospect of a living hope, the notion of God's promise in the midst of what they were experiencing, and probably would experience in the days ahead.

Peter stopped to remind the people of God that in the midst of all of life's deformities and weaknesses, brokenness and despair, all of it was really only temporary and that theirs was a living hope. And we can live today (and tomorrow) with the very same assurance. We can anticipate with a living hope that what God has in store for us is better than everything we've gone through.

A living hope lets you and me know that the best is not behind us, but ahead of us, that what's to come is better than what's been. A living hope can put a smile in our hearts and joy in our souls. A living hope can give us peace, and let us live with inner strength because we know that our tomorrows will be dramatically different than our todays.

I don't know who or what disappoints you, who or what has hurt or wounded you, who or what has defeated you, who or what has tried to bring you down and take you out this year.

But I do know that whatever it may have been, you can take heart in knowing that God has better things in store for you in the days ahead.

I encourage you to live in the New Year with the courage and hope of knowing that whatever it is, *"if God be for us, who (in the world) can be against us?"* Live with hope knowing that *"greater is He that is in (us) than he that is in the world."* (1 John 4:4) Live rejoicing, knowing that anything that seeks to degrade you, limit you or afflict you is only a temporary condition.

Better is on the way for you in 2015. So, live today with the courage God gives you. Live hoping, believing and trusting in Christ. And I guarantee that if you have a living hope in Christ, you can deal with your past and your present (whatever it is), because God has your future in God's hands.

So live singing -

"My hope is built… On nothing less…
Than Jesus's blood and righteousness.
I dare not trust the sweetest frame…
but wholly lean on Jesus's name.
On Christ, the solid rock I (we) stand…
All other ground is sinking sand."
("My Hope is Built")

-20-

HOPE IN CHANGING TIMES (REVISITED)

(This lecture was given at Grace United Methodist Church in Tacoma Park, MD on Monday, January 21, 2013 on the occasion of the second Inauguration of President Barack Obama as the 44th President of the United States and the annual celebration of Rev. Dr. Martin Luther King, Jr.'s birthday.)

Today, we celebrate the 84th anniversary of the birth of the Rev. Dr. Martin Luther King, Jr., and we share in the momentous and historic occasion of the Inauguration of President Barack Hussein Obama on his re-election as the 44th President of the United States of America.

As it regards Dr. King, among other things, he was an African-American Baptist preacher from Georgia who shook the foundations of American society. Dr. King's faith in God is to be viewed as inseparable from his hope of *Beloved Community* – a hope that he perpetually sought to convey to all of humanity.

For King, *Beloved Community* was intricately connected with the notion of hope. Christian hope served as the foundation for his vision of *Beloved Community*. In one of his later sermons, "The Meaning of Hope," King defined hope as that quality which is "necessary for life." (Baker-Fletcher, 132)

He asserted that hope was to be viewed as "animated and undergirded by faith and love." In his mind, if you had hope, you had faith in something. Thus, hope shares the belief that "all reality hinges on moral foundations." (Baker-Fletcher)

For King, hope was the refusal to give up "despite overwhelming odds." Hope beckons us to love everybody – both our enemies and allies. Hope helps us to see that we can resist giving up on one another because our lives together are animated by the belief that God is present in and with each and every one of us.

In his famous "I Have a Dream" speech delivered in our Nation's Capital in the summer of 1963 (almost 50 years ago), Dr. King shared that a part of his dream was that we would be able "to hew out of the mountain of despair, a stone of hope."

These are days of tremendous change and challenge in our society. From the collapse of the economy that has affected all of us – to the wars that are now still being fought in at least two places in our world – to the proliferation of violence that affects too many of our communities - to the healthcare crisis that still results in millions of Americans still living without affordable, adequate healthcare – to the ever-expanding prison industrial complex, where we are reminded by Dr. Michelle Alexander in her book, *The New Jim Crow* that we have more black and brown men in prison than we do in college - indeed, these are days of unprecedented and tremendous change and challenge.

Barack Obama and Hope Revisited

Amidst these challenges, the historic presidency of Barack Obama, our first president of African descent, continues to be a sign of hope for many persons across the nation and the world. While Obama's first election in 2008 renewed hope for many of us, we recall that his candidacy also offered a vivid snapshot of the state of race relations then.

We recall that much of the political discourse leading up to President Obama's first election focused on his race, and questions about whether the nation was ready for a black president. Notice that these questions were raised almost 400 years after the first African slaves arrived on what would become America's shores, and almost 150 years after the legal abolition of slavery and emancipation of slaves in America.

One of the things that seemed to be lost in 2008 in the discourse surrounding Obama's candidacy is the fact that then Senator Obama was a highly qualified presidential candidate who rose from an impoverished upbringing in a single-parent home to become a person of exemplary achievement as a graduate of two Ivy League institutions (Columbia and Harvard Universities), as a community organizer, and as a state legislator in Illinois.

During his campaign for re-election last year, America in many ways again showed its ugliness as it became more and more apparent that race continues to matter in America, and that we are not yet close to being the post-racial or post-racist society that we may aspire to become. We recall that during the most recent presidential campaign, the racial divide was coded in images and terms like an "empty chair" and "invisibility", the "47 percent", which candidates were and were not concerned about the very poor among us, and the insinuation that Obama was sharing gifts and entitlements with persons along race lines. Today, it is clear that race continues to matter in America.

In his 2006 book, *The Audacity of Hope*, Obama himself offered words of caution to America in thinking that we may have arrived at becoming "post-racial" or that we already live in a color-blind society, and that we may be beyond the need for constructive discourse and critical engagement as it regards racism and related forms of oppression and injustice in America. Obama wrote:

> To say that we are one people is not to suggest that race no longer matters – that the fight for equality has been won, or that the problems that minorities face in this country today are largely self-inflicted. We know the statistics: On almost every single socioeconomic indicator, from infant mortality to life expectancy to employment to home ownership, black and Latino Americans in particular lag far behind their white counterparts. (Obama 2006, 232)

Certainly, realizing hope is not easy. In his 2008 book, *Hope on a Tightrope*, philosopher Cornel West lays the groundwork for a discourse on hope in its contemporary context. Dr. West states: "Real hope is grounded in a particularly messy struggle and it can be betrayed by naive projections of a better future that ignores the necessity of doing the real work." (West, *Hope on a Tightrope,* 6)

However, I believe that the re-election of Barak Obama offers glimmers of hope for many in America and around the world - that someday we might be the *Beloved Community* of which Dr. Martin Luther King, Jr. dreamt. The vision of Dr. King and President Obama were not dissimilar. They both offer us a framework – a roadmap - for what Obama has termed an audacity of hope. Fundamentally this is a hope – like Mohandas Gandhi's hope – that is grounded in our individual and collective willingness to become the change that we seek in the world.

Hope and the Beloved Community Revisited

Indeed, this historic day is in part a realization of the dream that Dr. Martin Luther King, Jr. talked about on the steps of the Lincoln Memorial almost 50 years ago. In the final analysis, Dr. King's dream was rooted in hope for all of humanity. His hope for humanity – his hope for every neighborhood and every hamlet – his hope for every child – black, white, brown and red - was grounded in his belief in our God-given potential to live as the *Beloved Community.*

King asserted that "all life is interrelated." One of his fundamental beliefs was in the kinship of all persons. He believed all life is part of a single process; all living things are interrelated; and all persons are sisters and brothers. All of us have a place in the *Beloved Community.*

Near the end of his life, Dr. King published a book entitled, *Where Do We Go from Here: Chaos or Community?* In it, King reiterated a point he had made on several other occasions. He pointed out that we are faced with a choice in our life together, and that we will either learn to live together as brothers and sisters, or we will die together as fools. Society today looks quite different from the society of 40 years ago. Progress can be seen in many areas, thus giving us the framework for hope upon which we might build.

Is There a Balm?

On numerous occasions, Dr. Martin Luther King, Jr. pointed out that the nature of hope is evident in questions posed by the prophet Jeremiah –

"Is there no balm in Gilead; is there no physician there? Why then has the health of my poor people not been restored?" (Jeremiah 8:22)

King intimated that amidst the oppression that many had experienced in America – people of faith in God were able to convert the *question marks* of the prophet Jeremiah's lament, into *exclamation points* as they affirmed their faith and hope in the living and life-giving God. And so they sang with blessed assurance:

There is a balm in Gilead,
to make the wounded whole
There is a balm in Gilead,
To heal the sin-sick soul.
Sometimes I feel discouraged,
And think my work's in vain

And then the Holy Spirit
Revives my soul again! (Songs of Zion, 123)

Hope for a better future is ultimately rooted and grounded in our shared potential and commitment to change the world and make it better. Finally, Dr. King shared that everybody can be great because everybody can serve. He further shared that our service is the rent that we pay for the space that we occupy on earth. Let us be hopeful that each of those who today around this nation and the globe celebrate Dr. Martin Luther King, Jr.'s life and President Barack Obama's inauguration will be committed to paying some rent.

-21-

FINDING COMMON GROUND FOR THE COMMON GOOD

(This presentation was first delivered at the Ecumenical Institute of Theology, St. Mary's Seminary University, Baltimore, MD on April 9, 2013, as one of three theological responses to a lecture delivered by Rev. Jim Wallis on "Finding Common Ground for the Common Good," on the occasion of the publication of Wallis's book entitled, "On God's Side.".)

I would venture to suggest that at the root of Protestantism is an ongoing quest for an appropriation of the common good. Martin Luther's call for the reformation of the church in the 16th century seemed to signal a call for Christian communities to address matters of ecclesial, theological, and socio-political significance to the masses of people. By its very nature Reformation faith and Protestantism served as a faithful protest against what was perceived – at least to some degree – as the class abuses of the church and society – directed primarily at the poor. In as much as the Protestant Reformation was to become a protest against some of the practices of the church - as perceived by Luther and others - it would also become a framework for reforming and reframing some of the practices of Christianity in the search for common ground and the common good.

The quest for such common good became one of the marks of enlightenment faith that would be the hallmark of early Protestantism in America. Martin Marty intimates in his book *Pilgrims in their Own Land* that although early 15th and 16th century settlers in the American colonies were largely "pilgrims of dissent," what they shared was a common quest for freedom, and that colonists were "knit together by law, religion, and custom." (Marty 1984, 75)

It seems that much of the quest for an appropriation of the common good in the late 19th and early 20th centuries can be viewed against the philosophical and ethical backdrop of utilitarianism. Although there continues to be a great deal of debate as to the merits of utilitarianism as a philosophical and ethical construct, at least in some measure, it was the thinking of Jeremy Bentham and John Stuart Mill, among others, that their notion of "utility" provided a framework to talk about what is good and what brings about the common good. Thus, a critical question of utilitarianism is, "What is it that brings about the "the greatest possible good for the greatest possible number of individuals?"

In the social teachings of virtually every American Protestant denomination, there has been (and continues to be) an expressed concern for the common good. For instance, in foundational documents of the Presbyterian, Episcopal and Lutheran churches, among other Protestant denominations, there are statements which point to concerns for the common good within the denominations themselves, within the context of the churches' ecumenical and interfaith relations, and within the context of the broader society.

In the Methodist churches/denominations – which I am most familiar - the theology and practice of communality and common good finds a primary point of reference at the place of social holiness – where the concern for vital piety and commnal religious practice is coupled with concerns for acts of mercy and justice – as seen in social witness, societal engagement and concern for the common good. Thus, a primary theological mandate of churches/denominations in the Wesleyan tradition was and has continued to be "to reform the nation and spread scriptural holiness."

In much of American Christianity, and certainly in the Protestantism of the early and mid-20th century, there continued to be a clear quest for an appropriation of the common good. This is seen perhaps most clearly in an articulation of the Social Gospel by Walter Rauschenbusch. In his seminal work, *A Theology of the Social Gospel*, Rauschenbusch states that "we have a social gospel." (Rauschenbusch 1945, 1)

For Rauschenbusch, the Gospel, by its very nature is "social" and has communal implications. His ministry and work in New York City laid the foundation for a clear movement in many Protestant circles in the mid-20th century toward the predominance of evangelical liberalism – as also espoused by the likes of Howard Thurman. Like Rauschenbusch, Thurman would assert that the Gospel by its very nature is "social" and concerned with the common good.

In one of his works, which he titled, *The Search for Common Ground*, Thurman argued that the search for common ground is a universal search among all of humanity.

He stated that "A person is always threatened in one's very ground by a sense of isolation, by feeling oneself cut off from one's fellows. Yet, the person can never separate oneself from one's fellows, for mutual interdependence is characteristic of all life." (Thurman 1971, 2-3) Thus, for Thurman, this common, universal quest and search for common ground has teleological implications, as it essentially provides the framework for the meaning of life itself.

Thurman's articulation of a "search for common ground" would ultimately serve as one of the primary theoretical precursors to the work of Dr. Martin Luther King, Jr. and King's articulation of a vision of "beloved community" which became the theological grounding for the Civil Rights movement in America, and subsequent human rights movements – and the quest for common ground – around the world.

Interestingly, in one of his chapters in *On God's Side*, Jim Wall posits that "The Beloved Community Welcomes All Tribes." (Wallis, 109) Wallis shares a quote from King that "our goal is to create a beloved community and this will require a qualitative change in our souls as well as a quantitative change in our lives."

Again, it is important to note that the singular theological and societal vision of Martin Luther King, Jr. was for the realization of *Beloved Community*. Kenneth Smith and Ira Zepp, Jr. in their seminal 1974 work entitled, *Search for the Beloved Community,* suggested that King's perspective on the Christian love-ethic provides critical insight into understanding his persistent search for the

Beloved Community. For King, it was rooted in the biblical notion of *Agape* (God's unconditional love), and was to be the ultimate goal for society. (Smith and Zepp 1974, 129-156)

King asserted that "all life is interrelated." One of his fundamental beliefs was in the kinship of all persons. He believed that all life is part of a single process; all living things are interrelated; and all persons are sisters and brothers. (Baker-Fletcher 1993, 132) All have a place in the *Beloved Community.* Because all life is interrelated, one cannot harm another without harming oneself. King elaborated:

> To the degree that I harm my brother, no matter what he is doing to me, to that extent I am harming myself. For example, white men often refuse federal aid to education in order to avoid giving the Negro his rights; but because all men are brothers, they cannot deny Negro children without harming themselves. Why is this? Because all men are brothers. If you harm me, you harm yourself. Love, *agape*, is the only cement that can hold this broken community together. When I am commanded to love, I am commanded to restore community, to resist injustice, and to meet the needs of my brothers. (Baker-Fletcher)

I want to suggest that much of what was articulated and in-fact appropriated as the common good through the middle of the 20th century has been obscured at the least, and at worst has been lost and forgotten. Perhaps as a reflection of society in general, churches today seem to have become more inwardly focused - religion and faith have become increasingly privatized and insular. As a result, forms of external religious expression like ecumenism, interreligious and interfaith dialogue and engagement, and the capacity of churches to critically engage culture and society in the public square have, in large measure, been diminished.

And so what might be some things to consider in a turn back toward common concern, and toward a common quest for common ground and the common good?

Imperative

Howard Thurman and Martin Luther King, Jr. were among those who spoke to the divine and moral imperative – the calling - that Christians share in seeking common ground, the common good and *Beloved Community*. This imperative – this calling - is rooted and grounded in a divine commitment to advance the appropriation of the Christian love-ethic as foundational for constructively moving toward the realization of authentic community and the common good. Thurman asserted that God's intent is for the human family to live in community as interrelated members. Jesus came into the world to call persons back into community.

An imitation of the unconditional love revealed in the life and teachings of Jesus can be helpful in the quest for common ground and common good. Moving toward a deeper sense of who we are as individuals and community will enable us to live more shalom-filled lives, modeled on the life of Christ. There is the obligation to treat every person as Christ Himself, respecting her/his life as if it were the life of Christ.

Inspiration

In *Jesus and the Disinherited,* Howard Thurman asserted that Jesus was acutely aware of the cultural context of his ministry. (see Thurman 1952, 11-35) Jesus knew that his teachings regarding God's justice, love, mercy, forgiveness and peace would cause controversy and get him into trouble with the religious and political authorities of his day. Yet, he remained faithful to his mission, and sought to perpetually live the God-inspired message that he had been given.

For the church, the appropriation of community as a transformational Christ-centered, Spirit-filled process needs to be understood within the context of God's ongoing work in salvation history. The development of common ground for the common good thus requires God-connectedness through the inspiration of the Holy Spirit.

Like Christ, it has been suggested that Howard Thurman was a "God intoxicated man," and as such offered a paradigm of God-centered and God-inspired ministry. Perhaps, it is the case today that Christians are beckoned to live likewise in a "God-intoxicated" way, as we seek to bring about the common good among us.

Integration

The quest for common ground and the common good is at the heart of the church's ministry. The church, the gathering of believers who confess Christ as Lord, is an embodiment of community and common good over history. For this reason, the church is called to model community and must help the world achieve common ground, while believing that unity among human beings is possible – and community is fully evident - only if there is real justice for all people.

A commitment to the realization of the common good offers real hope for the world in which we live. Jims Wallis points to the UBUNTU theology of Desmond Tutu as practiced during the fight against Apartheid in South Africa as being a sign of hope for a movement toward appropriating (and re-appropriating) the common good in the 21st century. UBUNTU is a Zulu term that speaks to the quality of being human that is imbedded in all of humanity – by virtue of the fact that we are all human. UBUNTU thus binds us together as a human family. It essentially states that, "I am because you are, and because you are, therefore, I am".

UBUNTU speaks to the yearning toward community. Community – common ground – by its very nature - is integrative; it speaks to a "common unity" among us. Authentic community includes persons of different races, sexes, ages, religions, cultures, viewpoints, lifestyles, and stages of development - and serves to integrate persons into a whole that is greater – more actualized and dynamic – than the sum of its parts. Forms of disintegration and disunity are, therefore, to be understood as being antithetical to the common good, community and to the will of God.

I appreciate that Rev. Jim Wallis concludes his provocative work, *On God's Side* by pointing us towards grace – and in-fact the amazing grace of God. It is my sense that this quest, this striving for common good, as it is to be realized, must be filled with the grace of God. For as John Newton intimated in his great hymn, "Amazing Grace," … "Grace has brought us safe thus far, and grace shall lead us on."

-22-

PRAYER FOR THE STATE OF MARYLAND

(This prayer was delivered as the Invocation to open the session of the Maryland State Senate on February 24, 2014 in Annapolis, Maryland.)

O God, you are the creator of all that is and is to be. We are created by you, for service to you and with each other. Today, we take this opportunity to offer prayers for the great state of Maryland, for our nation and the world. We pray for the people of every city and county of this state. We pray for the younger and the older persons among us. We pray for the peace and safety of all of our communities, for every home and every street.

Lord God, we pray for your blessings upon all persons, and especially upon those who bear the burdens of want and disparity among us - whether it be for lack of food, clean water or shelter, inadequate healthcare or substandard education.

We pray for all persons who serve in elective and appointive office on the state, local and national levels. Grant each of them a significant portion of wisdom and compassion, that through their service among us, all of your people across this state will prosper. O God, hear our prayers as only you can, and bless us as only you will. Amen.

-23-

BECOMING A TRANSFORMED NONCONFORMIST (the re-mix)

(This was the Commencement Address for the Wesley Theological Seminary Course of Study School at Metropolitan Memorial United Methodist Church in Washington, DC on July 29, 2014.)

***"Be not conformed to this world; but be transformed by the renewing of your mind."* (Romans 12:2)**

First, I would like to express appreciation to Dr. Douglas Powe for the very kind invitation to share with you on this momentous occasion. And to Dr. Robert Martin, Dr. David McAllister-Wilson and all who are a part of the Wesley Theological Seminary community, I would like to say "thank you." It is quite an honor for me to return to the place that has been one of my spiritual and intellectual homes – a place where I have been a student, have served as a member of the Board of Governors, and have had the opportunity to occasionally teach over the years. And to the graduates of the 2014 class of the Wesley Theological Seminary Course of Study School, I offer words of congratulations and blessing to you, your families and the churches you serve.

I am reminded of the story of the two little boys who couldn't stay out of trouble (any trouble they could get into, they did). Their parents – frustrated that they could not get the boys to behave – decided to take them to see the pastor of their church. The pastor had the younger of the two boys come into the office first, and began to query him, "Tell me, where is God…?", he asked the boy several times, "Where is God…?" The boy, now frightened, got up and took off running out of the pastor's office to his house, and went up to his bedroom and hid in the closet. His big brother followed him home and found him in the closet, and asked him what had happened in the pastor's office to make him so afraid. The little boy replied, "I'm not sure, but God is missing, and the pastor thinks that you and I stole God."

In a world wrought with political, social and economic upheaval – a world troubled by war and terror – many people today are asking, "where is God?" And it is a part of our vocation as pastors and leaders to help people in the church and the world locate God.

About fifty years ago, Rev. Dr. Martin Luther King, Jr. preached a sermon entitled, "Transformed Nonconformist." Dr. King based his message on the familiar text from the apostle Paul's letter to the Roman Church, where in the 12th chapter, Paul reminded the Christians in Rome that they were to *"be not conformed to this world, but to be transformed by the renewing of (their) mind(s)."*

The context for Dr. King's message in addressing this matter of transformed nonconformity was the American Civil Rights movement of the mid-20th century, and the need for adaptive, transformational leadership in the church and society that would stay the course in seeking to transform society and deliver America from the racial division, economic disparity, and other social and political maladies that plagued our nation then.

Dr. King's message has intrigued and haunted me over the years, as I have thought about what it means to be a leader in the church. And it has led me lately to think about what it means for us to be adaptive and transformational in our leadership. In a nutshell, adaptive leadership is what I sense King was talking about when he talked about transformed nonconformity.

And who better to turn to than the apostle Paul in thinking on matters of adaptation and transformation? Indeed, Paul knew something about transformed nonconformity. He knew something about "adaptive leadership" before it became one of the new buzz-phrases in the contemporary church and business worlds.

Paul was the embodiment of adaptation and transformation. He was a Jewish Pharisee who would be touched by Jesus and would become a Christian convert. He was a Judeo-Christian, a born-again believer, a lawyer, a theologian, a philosopher and a new church start pastor. Paul preached to Jews and Gentiles, the richer and the poorer, the haves, the have nots and the have mores.

He was practical and systematic, pastoral and prophetic. If there was anybody who modeled transformed nonconformity and adaptive leadership, and practiced what he preached, it was the apostle Paul.

Paul said, *"don't be conformed to (don't try to be like) this world, but be transformed (be changed) by the renewing (the changing) of your mind(s)."*

Hear Eugene Peterson's re-mix on this verse from the *Message* translation of the Bible: "*Don't be so well-adjusted to your culture that you fit into it without thinking. Instead, fix your attention on God. You'll be changed from the inside out.*"

Concerning this matter of conformity and the call to transformation, Dr. King wrote in his sermon decades ago these words, "Success, recognition and conformity are the bywords of the modern world where everyone seems to crave the anesthetizing security of being identified with the majority... In spite of the prevailing tendency to conform, we as Christians have a mandate to be nonconformists."

Adaptation and transformation are the primary leadership challenges for the 21st century church and its leaders. In this nanosecond, drive-through, instant message, instant everything world in which we live, it is our challenge as leaders to lead in changing the realities in our churches and communities in ways that make sense for today. And we must lead in ways where we are not subsumed by every fad, quick-fix, church guru, church consultant and coach (many of whom haven't transformed and grown churches themselves), every program, seminar, workshop, conference, webinar, podcast and great idea that comes along.

As transformed nonconformists, we must be prayerful and discerning, discreet and strategic in determining what will be needed to lead our churches and communities towards the specific vision - the preferred future - that God intends. We must resist the temptation to keep up with the "ecclesial Jones," and to copy and imitate every apparently successful mega-church, big-church, Bentley-driving preacher that comes along.

We must be pastoral and theological, love everybody while listening to them and leading them, and stay true to the Gospel while relating (not conforming) to a super-fast-changing world. Ours must be the life of the re-mix – changing, growing, shifting, improvising, adapting and transforming – but never conforming.

To conform means that we remain mired in the mess in our midst, but to transform means that we're about the business of helping to re-form, re-mold, re-make and re-mix the mess that's around us into something new.

Indeed, it is the adaptive, transformational leader's task to speak truth and change where there is un-health and dis-ease in the church and society, lead in transforming current reality where necessary, and honor, celebrate and build on those places and spaces where the church and God's people are healthy and growing.

And we know that adaptive leadership – transformed nonconformity - is not easy. Paul, said "you" be not conformed, and "you" be transformed by the renewing of "your" mind. He didn't say that the *church* needs to be transformed, or that the *denomination* needs to be transformed, or even that the *world* needs to be transformed, but that "you" (and I) must be transformed.

I am reminded of another story of two elderly people who went out on a date. While on the date, the man asked the woman to marry him. At the end of the evening, he took his date home, and by the time he had arrived at his house, he had forgotten what her response was to his marriage proposal. So he called his date, and asked, “Did I ask you to marry me tonight, and if so, what was your response?” Her reply was, “I’m glad you called, because I knew I said “yes” to somebody, but I had forgotten who it was.”

We’ve always got to remember to whom it is that we have said “yes”.

Indeed, if the church and society are to be transformed in this present day, if change is to occur around us, it will have to begin in and with us. Paul implored, ““You” be transformed by the renewing of “your” mind.” Mohandas Gandhi told the people of India in the midst of their revolutionary struggle for change and liberation, that they were, “to be the change (they) want to see in the world.” In other words, if we want to see the change – we need to be the change.

Indeed, it has taken persons like the apostle Paul and Rev. Dr. Martin Luther King, Jr. to show us what adaptive, transformational leadership looks like. It has been persons like Rev. John Wesley and Bishop Leontine Kelly who have led the way over history in showing us what it means to be adaptive and transformational leaders.

And now… it’s up to you and me.

-24-

A PRAYER FOR THE STATE OF MARYLAND

(This prayer was delivered as the Invocation to open the Maryland State Senate Session in Annapolis, Maryland on March 4, 2015.)

God of our weary years, God of our silent tears; thou who has brought us thus far along the way. Thou who has by thy might, led us into the light - keep us forever in thy path we pray.
(James Weldon Johnson)

O God, you see all and know all – and we thank you for the privilege of gathering together again. Amidst the adverse weather of winter and the other challenges that many of your people face, we are mindful that you are in control of all that is and is to be.

We pray that you will bless each of those who serve the great state of Maryland in elected and appointed office with your wisdom and compassion. God of peace and justice, we pray that your justice will roll down as waters, and your righteousness as an ever-flowing stream (Amos 5:24).

Wherever we find ourselves, help us to be mindful that we all belong to you. Guide and protect your people, from the youngest to the oldest among us, and let us remember that each of us is an instrument created by you to carry out your plan for the world. God, may your mighty and divine hand reach across our state and nation, and touch every home and hamlet, every school and every institution. Bless your people wherever we are, and make your presence forever known and felt among us. Amen.

-25-
GOT HOPE!
ADDRESS TO THE UNITED METHODIST LEGAL FORUM

(This address was delivered in Baltimore, Maryland on May 2, 2015.)

"...and we boast in our hope of sharing the glory of God... knowing that our suffering produces endurance, and endurance produces character, and character produces hope, and hope does not disappoint us..." (Romans 5:1-5)

This week has been filled with tumult and turmoil just in our backyard here in Baltimore. We've experienced the very public funeral of Mr. Freddie Gray. We've witnessed the lashing out of many of our of young people - and some not so young - some of whom have expressed their anger, frustration and outrage by looting Mondawmin Mall – just a few miles from where we now are in Baltimore.

We've witnessed looting and destruction of several drug stores and food markets – and the destruction and burning of houses, cars and church property. We've witnessed lashing out with violence against police officers. We've seen the presence of the Maryland National Guard planted down in the city with the stated purpose of maintaining order on the city's streets.

We've experienced a city-wide curfew, and we've witnessed numerous people arrested. And amidst all of this, there were at least five more people murdered in Baltimore, and at least 12 more people shot this past week – with one of those who were murdered being a close friend of the late Mr. Freddie Gray. We've seen city and state officials wrestle with what would be the best course of action to bring about peace and a sense of justice for Mr. Freddie Gray's family, for the Sandtown-Winchester community, for zip code 21217, and for the city of Baltimore.

The eyes of the entire nation and world have been trained on Baltimore. We've seen and experienced what has appeared to be hopelessness.

And in the midst of all of this – we have also seen many people come together to pray for peace. We've seen people come together to march in peaceful protest. We've seen people come together to begin the work of rebuilding Baltimore, a city torn by destruction and decay over many decades. We've seen churches open their doors to feed the hungry, and provide safe-havens for children. We've seen some people celebrate at the announcement that criminal charges would be brought against those police officers alleged to have been responsible for the death of Mr. Gray.

We have seen members of the Baltimore Symphony Orchestra leave their music halls in the midst of the rioting to offer beautiful music on the streets of the city. We've seen phenomenal acts of generosity and kindness. So, in the midst of all that we've gone through this past week – through it all – we realize that we've still got hope.

The days, times and conditions in which the apostle Paul ministered were probably, in many ways, not unlike what we are experiencing today. In Rome, there was an apparent paucity of hope – even among the people who had come to know of the living Christ. An apparent paucity of hope is what the Apostle Paul was preaching to here. Maybe, this paucity of hope was due to the existence of severe persecution of the people in the church because of their beliefs in Christ, and maybe it was also because of the very real challenges that they faced in their daily living.

In many ways, the church today is well-acquainted with those realities that challenge our hopefulness both within and outside the church. Indeed, an inventory of our world and the church gives clear indication that we teeter (and teeter) on the brink of hopelessness and despair – with wars that have lasted far too long and killed way too many, violence in too many of our neighborhoods, increasing gaps between the have-gots and the have-nots, matters that threaten to divide the churches and our communities. We teeter on the brink of hopelessness.

And yet, if the church has been, and is to be anything, we are to be that people who boldly embodies hope. This was Paul's very point in his words to the Christians in Rome –

"...and we boast in our hope of sharing the glory of God... knowing that our suffering produces endurance, and endurance produces character, and character produces hope, and hope does not disappoint us..." (Romans 5:4-5)

Hope is real, and should be real to you and me. Rev. Dr. Martin Luther King, Jr. defined Christian hope as that quality which is "necessary for life.' King asserted that hope was to be viewed as "animated and undergirded by faith and love." In his mind, if you had hope, you had faith in something. Thus, for him, hope shares the belief that "all reality hinges on moral foundations." For King, hope was the refusal to give up "despite overwhelming odds." (Baker-Fletcher, 232)

Hope is real, and should be real to you and me. When talking about hope, St. Augustine of Hippo stated that, "Hope has two beautiful daughters; their names are Anger and Courage. Anger at the way things are, and Courage to see that they do not remain as they are." Hope is rooted in both the awareness that change is needed, and the courage to act so that change will occur.

Hope assures us *that "justice will roll down as waters, and righteousness as a mighty stream."* (Amos 5:24) Hope gives us the confidence that peace will come, and that change is indeed on the way.

We've got hope! One of the things I've learned about hope is that there are times when we tend to trivialize and even mythologize hope so much so that we might not recognize it even when it is in our midst. I say this to suggest that if we take time to look around, we will see hope all around us.

Children laughing and playing, that's hope. Music in our ears, that's hope. Food on our tables, that's hope.

Clothes on our backs and shoes on our feet, that's hope. A roof over our heads, that's hope. New awakenings and new beginnings, that's hope!

And so, whatever our lot today, as people in and of Christ, we've got hope! And let me remind us what hope really is. Hope is in the name of Jesus. Hope lets us wake up knowing – *"morning by morning new mercies I see"*. (Lamentations 3:23) Hope lets us lie down at night knowing that *"weeping may endure for a night, but joy comes in the morning"*. (Psalm 30:5) Hope reminds us that *"faith is the substance of things hoped for, and the evidence of things not seen"*. (Hebrews 11:1)

Hope is what Rev. Charles Albert Tindley knew about when he sang -

> "I do not know how long 'twill be
> Or what the future holds for (you or) me
> But this I know
> If Jesus leads (us),
> (We'll) get home, someday…"

We've Got Hope!

-26-

GOT HOPE! (REVISITED)

(This sermon was preached at Epworth Chapel, Baltimore, MD in May 2015 in the aftermath of the death of Mr. Freddie Gray in Baltimore.)

"Therefore, since we have been justified through faith, we have peace with God through our Lord Jesus Christ, through whom we have gained access by faith into this grace in which we now stand. And we boast in the hope of the glory of God. Not only so, but we also glory in our sufferings, because we know that suffering produces perseverance; perseverance, character; and character, hope. And hope does not put us to shame, because God's love has been poured out into our hearts through the Holy Spirit, who has been given to us. (Romans 5:1-5)

The apostle Paul is a fascinating study in church leadership for any number of reasons. In his day, Paul would have been considered what we now call an adaptive leader – not conformed to his time and the people around him – but transformed by the renewing that had occurred in him. As a pastor, preacher, theologian, lawyer and new church planter – Paul indeed is a compelling study of one who in the midst of the hardships and trials of his time – was encouraged to keep at the task of preaching the Gospel, and to also keep at the task of encouraging those in the churches that he had planted to never give up.

The days, times and conditions in which Paul ministered were probably in many ways not unlike what we are experiencing today. In Rome, there was an apparent paucity of hope – even among the people who had come to know of the living Christ. An apparent paucity of hope is what the Apostle was preaching to here. Maybe it was due to the existence of severe persecution of the people in the church because of their beliefs in Christ, and maybe it was also because of the very real challenges that they faced in their daily living.

In many ways, the church today is well-acquainted with those realities both within and outside the church that challenge our hopefulness. Indeed, an inventory of our world and the church gives us a clear indication that we teeter (and teeter) on the brink of hopelessness and despair – with wars that have lasted far too long and killed way too many, violence in too many of our neighborhoods, increasing gaps between the "have-gots" and the "have-nots", and matters that continue to threaten to divide the churches. We teeter (and teeter) on the brink of hopelessness.

And yet, if the church has been and is to be anything, we are to be the people who boldly embody hope. This was Paul's very point in his words to the Christians in Rome –

"*...and we boast in our hope of sharing the glory of God... knowing that our suffering produces endurance, and endurance produces character, and character produces hope, and hope does not disappoint us...*" (Romans 5:4-5)

Hope is real, and should be real to you and me. Hope is what German theologian Jürgen Moltmann wrote about when he wrote – "Hope alone is to be called "realistic" because it alone takes seriously the possibilities with which all reality is fraught. Hope does not take things as they happen to stand or to lie, but as progressing, moving things with possibilities of change." (Moltmann 1993, 25)

Dr. Martin Luther King, Jr. defined Christian hope as that quality which is "necessary for life". King asserted that hope was to be viewed as "animated and undergirded by faith and love." In his mind, if you had hope, you had faith in something. Thus, for him, hope shares the belief that "all reality hinges on moral foundations." It was, for King, the refusal to give up "despite overwhelming odds." (Baker-Fletche 1953, 232)

We've got hope. One of the things I've learned about hope is that there are times when we tend to trivialize and even mythologize hope so much so that we may not recognize it even when it is in our midst. I say this to suggest that if we take time to look around, we will see hope all around us.

Children laughing and playing, that's hope! Music in our ears, that's hope! Food on our tables, clothes on our backs, shoes on our feet, new awakenings, that's hope! All of the ways that God has made for us in the past, that's hope!

And so whatever our lot today, as people in and of Christ, we've got hope! Whether we have or have not – we've got hope! Whether we are in joy or sorrow right now

– the good news is that as people of God's promise in Christ – we've got hope!

"I do not know how long 'twill be
Or what the future holds for me.
But this I know,
If Jesus leads (us),
(We'll) get home, someday…
(Charles Albert Tindley)

-27-

THE LONGEST NIGHT

(This address was delivered on December 20, 2015 at the Baltimore City Memorial Service for those who died from homelessness in 2015 in Baltimore.)

"… for I was hungry and you gave me food, I was thirsty and you gave me something to drink, I was a stranger and you welcomed me, I was naked and you gave me clothing, I was sick and you took care of me, I was in prison and you visited me… and 'Truly I tell you, just as you did it to one of the least of these, you did it to me.'" (Matthew25:41-45)

On this first night of winter, the longest and often one of the coldest nights of the year, we gather in solidarity with and for those in our city, state, nation and world who are forced to endure the night. We gather to remember those who this year and in years past have died while enduring the night.

The night, by nature, is supposed to be a point and place of rest and respite from the work of the day. The night is meant to be a place of peace, quiet and tranquility from daytime's hustle and bustle.

But for far too many of our sisters and brothers, the night is a place of prolonged agony and despair. The night is a place of dark want and desperate need, a place of painful isolation and luminous want. For too many persons in our city and state, the night is their home, the place where they are forced to lay their head, and wonder with seemingly perpetual dismay – how long will the night be, and wonder if it will ever end for them.

Elie Wiesel in his book entitled, *Night*, depicts night as embodying in its most hopeful dimension, a transition from darkness to light, filled with the promise of the beginning of a new day. But Wiesel wants us to see that there is too often a certain tragic irony and finality of the night that results in everything coming to an end. About *Night*, Wiesel wrote, "I wanted to show the end, the finality of the event. Everything came to an end – man, history, life and meaning. There was nothing left." This is the very fate of too many of our homeless sisters and brothers in Baltimore.

As we gather this evening in Baltimore – the largest city, in the wealthiest state in America - we gather amidst the very real contradictions of wealth and poverty – abundance and scarcity – among us. These contradictions affect every aspect of our lives together. Homelessness, the plight of the unhoused and housing insecure, is related to the scarcity that is found in lack all around us – scarcity of adequate healthcare, nutrition, education, employment, safety and transportation for those who have the least among us.

In Baltimore, the 5th most violent city in the nation, much of our attention continues to be focused on the gun violence and gang violence in our midst. But, Mohandas K. Gandhi intimated years ago that "poverty is the worst form of violence." It is incumbent upon us who are concerned about the plight of our unhoused, homeless neighbors, to see homelessness as in and of itself, inflicting violence upon its victims – violence on the soul and dignity of homeless persons, violence which affects their physical well-being and threatens their lives, violence which impacts the potential and possibility of individuals and society as a whole. It is incumbent upon those who are charged with establishing policy and setting political agendas to see the moral implications of homelessness.

Some of what underlies our will to such violence on the soul, and our inability or unwillingness to house all of the homeless persons among us is rooted in the very real and deep racial and class divides that exist among us, even in this city. Ta-Nehisi Coates in his book, *Between the World and Me*, writes about growing up on the streets of Baltimore, and states that "race is the child of racism, not the father." I'd add that class is the child of classism, not the mother. The twin evils of racism and classism serve as severe detriments to bringing about wholeness for those among us who find themselves living on the margins of our city.

In his book, *Jesus and the Disinherited,* Howard Thurman asks a haunting question (especially) for persons of faith. "What does Jesus of Nazareth have to say to those who have their backs against the wall?"

What does God have to say about the way the poor among us are treated?

> "... *for I was hungry and you gave me food, I was thirsty and you gave me something to drink, I was a stranger and you welcomed me, I was naked and you gave me clothing, I was sick and you took care of me, I was in prison and you visited me... and 'Truly I tell*

> *you, just as you did it to one of the least of these, you did it to me."* (Matthew 25:42-43)

Thurman offered a prayer that captures the existential darkness that we all may struggle with in seeking to do God's will –

In my confusion I shall often say the word that is not true and do the thing of which I am ashamed. There will be errors in the mind and great inaccuracies of judgment.

In seeking the light, I shall again and again find myself walking in the darkness.

I shall mistake my light for Your light and I shall drink from the responsibility of the choice I make.

Though my days be marked with failures, stumblings, fallings, let my spirit be free so that You may take it and redeem my moments in all the ways my needs reveal.

(Thurman, *The Mood of Christmas)*

In April 2002, Wiesel reflected on his experiences during the Holocaust and shared –

> "People say occasionally that there must be light at the end of the tunnel, but I believe in those times there was light in the tunnel. In a strange way there was courage in the ghetto, and there was hope, human hope, in the death camps. Simply an anonymous prisoner giving a piece of his bread to someone who was hungrier than he or she; a father

> shielding his child; a mother trying to hold back her tears so her children would not see her pain—that was courage."

Amidst the night, our divine and moral prerogative is to speak out and act out – individually and socially – with and for our neighbors - to speak out and act out in compassion and justice. Our divine and moral prerogative is to speak out and act out in ways that address the immediate needs of God's people who must endure the night – those on our city's margins - by providing shelter, food and clothing – while also addressing the serious systemic political, economic and moral concerns that lead us to ask why our sisters and brothers are forced to endure the night in the first place.

-28 –

ROAD RULES : LESSONS FROM THE JERICHO ROAD

(This sermon was preached at Wesley Theological Seminary in Washington, DC on February 2, 2016.)

But wanting to justify himself, he asked Jesus,
"And who is my neighbor?"
(Luke 10:29; 25-37)

In the city of Baltimore, where I do ministry, several communities have come to be designated and known as "Blue Light" neighborhoods. These are considered to be some of the most dangerous neighborhoods in the city, and at night one can see the constant blinking of blue lights overhead. These lights are a reminder of the crime and violence that has affected and often afflicted many of our communities and the people who live in them and travel through them. It is my sense that these "Blue Light" neighborhoods are not unlike the Jericho road that Jesus was speaking about in scripture.

Jesus uses what has come to be known as the story of the Good Samaritan to teach those of his day and teach those of us who would hear this story even today, some "road rules". The Jericho road was known to be a dangerous road

– a winding and dark road - where it was not unusual for people to experience the type of violence that Jesus points to in the story of the Good Samaritan.

It seems as though the times of Jesus were not much unlike ours. We are reminded of the arduous nature of some of the proverbial "roads of life" today.

Jesus offers the example of this certain unnamed man who had been beaten, stripped, robbed and left on the road to die. We are told that a priest and a Levite – for whatever reasons – chose to pass this beaten man by on the other side of the road. We don't know for sure, but perhaps they were on their way to important religious meetings, and knew that to stop and care for this certain man would have made them late for their religious commitments.

And lest you and I hold these two religious leaders of the Lord's day in too much disdain, let us remind ourselves of the ways that people in need today are passed by in our churches and society. Racism, classism and militarism continue to afflict the church and society. Crime and violence continue to permeate many of our streets. Poverty, hunger and the lack of adequate healthcare continue to afflict too many among us (still over 20 million persons have inadequate healthcare in America). If the truth is told, just like this certain man on the Jericho road, people are too often passed by on the roadsides of life today.

It is against this backdrop that Jesus seeks to teach some road rules. And so what are the some of the rules of the road that we need to attend to today?

Martin Luther King, Jr. helped us to address the question in a sermon that he preached at Riverside Church in New York on April 4, 1967 (49 years ago):

> On the one hand we are called to play the Good Samaritan on life's road side; but that is only the initial act. One day we must come to see that the whole Jericho road must be transformed so that men and women will not be constantly beaten and robbed as they make their journey on life's highway. True compassion is more than flinging a coin to a beggar; it is not haphazard and superficial. It comes to see that an edifice which produces beggars needs restructuring. (King, "Beyond Vietnam")

Social theorist, Michael Eric Dyson points out that King believed that charity was a poor substitute for justice. Charity alone is a hit-or-miss proposition; people who tire of giving stop doing so when they think they've done enough. Justice seeks to take the distracting and fleeting emotions out of giving. Justice does not depend on feeling to do the right thing. Justice depends on right action and sound thinking about the most helpful route to the best and most virtuous outcome. King understood, and embodied, this noble distinction. People who give money to the poor deserve praise; people who give their lives to the poor deserve honor. (Dyson 2008, 120)

As Christians, our road rules must be rooted in true compassion. True compassion is always coupled with justice, and challenges each of us in the church and society to move towards engaging in what Dr. Martin Luther King,

Jr. called forms of "creative altruism." This is altruism that makes concern for others the first law of life.

King indicated that Jesus revealed the meaning of this type of altruism in his parable about the Good Samaritan who was moved by compassion to care for "a certain man" who had been robbed and beaten on the Jericho road.

King asserted that the creative altruism of the Samaritan was *universal, dangerous and excessive*.

When we practice such creative altruism, we are led to not only offer a handout, but we ask why people need a handout in the first place. Such creative altruism not only offers help to the beggar, to the stripped and robbed among us, but questions the conditions that lead to poverty and violence in the first place.

But wanting to justify himself, he asked Jesus, "And who is my neighbor?" (Luke 10:29)

Through this parable, Jesus disclosed his definition of a neighbor. A neighbor is both Jew and Gentile; she/he is Russian and American; he/she is Muslim, Jewish and Christian; she/he is Native American, Hispanic, Asian, white and black. She/he is richer and poorer – left and right – conservative and liberal – Democratic, Republican and Independent. A neighbor is "any certain man or woman" – any person in need – on any of the numerous Jericho roads of life.

Perhaps, we can learn something today from the generous acts of the Good Samaritan.

Perhaps he sang a familiar song as he lent a helping hand:

> If I can help somebody as I travel along,
> If I can cheer somebody with a word or a song.
> If I can help somebody as they're living wrong,
> Then my living will not be in vain…
> ("If I Can Help Somebody")

-29-

A PRAYER FOR THE STATE OF MARYLAND

(This prayer was delivered as the Invocation to open the Maryland State senate session in Annapolis, Maryland on April 8, 2016.)

Gracious, all-loving and all-wise God, in the busyness of this day we pause to offer thanks to you. We come from various directions and locations; we come with divergent perspectives; we come with a diversity of hopes, dreams and visions. But we come acknowledging that we gather in the commonality that all persons share in you, the creator of the universe.

O God, we offer thanks to you for the great state of Maryland. Today, we take this opportunity to offer prayers for this state, for our nation and the world. We pray for the people of every city and county of this state. We pray that in the days ahead, you would bless every home and every community - every school and every place where your people gather for work or leisure. Bless those persons who are older and those who are younger. We pray for peace and safety for all of us who live and move throughout this state, and we pray likewise for communities like ours across our nation and around the world.

Lord God, we pray especially for your blessings upon those persons who bear the undue burdens of want and disparity among us - whether it be for lack of food or shelter, inadequate healthcare or inadequate education.

We pray that you will bless each of us gathered here. Most importantly, we ask your blessings upon those who serve and lead the state of Maryland in elective and appointive office. Bless each of them with a portion of wisdom, patience, integrity, justice and compassion. Bless each of those who serve and lead that they will be forever mindful of a collective commitment to lead and act in ways that facilitate the betterment of each person, each home, each school, each community, and each place of business in Maryland.

"Now drop thy still dews of quietness; let all of our strivings cease; take now from our souls the strain and the stress; and let our ordered lives confess; the beauty of your peace"

(Howard Thurman). Amen.

-30-

I'VE SEEN THE PROMISED LAND: THE LEGACY OF MARTIN LUTHER KING, JR. and PROPHETIC PREACHING

(This lecture was delivered at the Festival of Preaching at St. Mary's Seminary and University, Baltimore, MD on April 16, 2016.)

The preaching, public ministry and practice of public theology of Rev. Dr. Martin Luther King, Jr. offer us critical lenses through which we can look and see the prophetic role of the preacher in the twenty-first century. In as much as Dr. King was a Baptist preacher and pastor, along with being most known in the public sphere as the leader of the American Civil Rights movement, he was a public theologian bringing to bear his theological training on the social and political conditions of his time. For him, faith – what we believe about God, the universe and God's people – was to be acted out in ways that brought about not only spiritual growth, but social transformation.

This is to say that for King, if the church was to be the church, it would engage in prophetic witness that would bring its spiritual, social, economic and political resources to bear in ways that would affirm God's love, and be truly reconciling, redeeming, liberating and transforming.

In his preaching and praxis of ministry, King's own particular prophetic concerns were to address what he deemed to be the "triplets of evil" – racism, classism (economic inequality), and militarism (war). His witness would spawn a religious and social movement unparalleled in American history. The demand for racial and social justice in the South would be the impetus for concomitant social and political movements across a number of sectors of society:

- The roots of the struggle for women's rights (feminism and womanism), the rights of gays and lesbians, the rights of workers and the disabled, and the rights of immigrants of various hews of brown, red, yellow and black can be traced to the prophetic stance of Dr. King.

- It was King who espoused a form of nonviolent social resistance and direct action that would ultimately lead to the passage of the Civil Rights Act (1964) and the Voting Rights Act (1965) by the United States Congress.
- The epistemic foundations of affirmative action – however we might view it today – are rooted in King's prophetic vision of equality and justice throughout society.
- The American Civil Rights movement - led by Dr. King - served as an impetus and model of liberation and human rights movements across the globe – in Africa, Asia, Europe, and Central and South America.

Here, I will address the legacy of Dr. Martin Luther King, Jr., with particular focus on ways that preachers today might appropriate and re-appropriate prophetic preaching and praxis within the context of 21st century realities in the church and society. This analysis will entail three parts. First, a brief overview of prophetic preaching – what it is - will be offered. Second, an analysis of the spiritual, social and intellectual development of Martin Luther King, Jr. will be offered. Here the formative influences (roots) - familial, spiritual (the church), communal, and intellectual - on King's thought and praxis will be examined. Who and what in his development most influenced King? Thirdly, a brief analysis of King's preaching and prophetic witness will be offered with a focus on implications for the 21st century church. What might we glean from the preaching and praxis of King as we seek to effect change into the future?

1. AFFLICTING THE COMFORTABLE: PROPHETIC PREACHING AND PUBLIC THEOLOGY

What are we speaking of when we speak of prophetic preaching? When addressing the matter of the prophetic role of the preacher, several questions must be raised. How does the preacher speak to the church and society with a prophetic voice? From whence does the power and authority of the preacher come? From whence has the power and authority of the preacher been derived over history?

What are the words that will "afflict the comfortable" and speak truth to power? What words will speak to the systemic evils of the churches and the world, and lead persons of faith in Christ, and even those who may lack faith, toward social transformation and just action?

Is there a word from the Lord today that will adequately and relevantly speak to increasingly complex social concerns, and lead to the wholeness of individuals and communities?

What words from the Lord speak to disparities in education, employment, healthcare, housing, safety and technology? Is there a word from the Lord that speaks to drug trafficking and addiction, violence, gambling and abortion? Is there a word from the Lord that speaks to gender injustice, marriage inequality, human trafficking, misogyny toward girls and women, domestic violence, police brutality, homelessness, war, terrorism (domestic and foreign) global warming, environmental injustice, white supremacy, over-incarceration, conspicuous consumption, materialism and greed?

What resources can the preacher today draw upon to empower her or him to speak to the abject poverty, racism, sexism and classism incumbent across much of society and extant in many of our communities?

Is there a word from the Lord about Ferguson, Mo, Charleston, SC, Cleveland, OH, Chicago, IL, Flint, MI, and Baltimore, MD? How might the preacher speak to the death inflicted upon the likes of Trayvon Martin, Michael Brown,

Sandra Bland, Tamir Rice, Koryn Gaines, Eric Garner and Freddie Gray?

What happens when the preacher is accused of mixing politics and religion? How can she/he preach in the legacy and tradition of the likes of Jarena Lee and Martin Luther King, Jr... Fannie Lou Hamer and Adam Clayton Powell... Katie Canon and Jeremiah Wright?

Should it ever be the preacher's role to speak to any issues of social and political concern, or are preachers only to speak of spiritual and pastoral matters? How might preachers today balance their pastoral and priestly roles with prophetic functions in preaching?

When speaking of prophetic preaching, we are essentially speaking of preaching which calls persons and structures back into relationship with God, and preaching that paves the way for the coming kin-dom of God.

Prophetic preaching is rooted in the Old Testament biblical traditions, and in the public ministries of the likes of John the Baptist and Jesus. It was generally the task of biblical prophets to speak to real conditions which existed among Hebrew people – and to call people back into covenant relationship with God. Thus, the biblical prophets stood with one foot in the past – reminding Israel of its history in God – and with one foot in the future, reminding people of their current spiritual and social condition, and of God's promise and hope for them. Prophets had one foot in the religious community, and the other foot in the public square. Thus, the paradigm for the biblical prophetic preacher is a dialectical paradigm of history and hope – past, present and future.

Prophetic preaching speaks holistically to the existential concerns of people and communities. It speaks to the hurts and hopes, and ultimately it challenges the status quo with the expectation of liberation from oppression and deliverance for God's people.

Marvin McMickle, in *Where have All the Prophets Gone?,* asserts that prophetic preaching shifts the focus of a congregation from what is happening as a local church to what is happening to them as a part of society. McMickle asserts that there is a need to recover this prophetic tradition in light of four prevailing trends in much of preaching today -

- An unclear/narrow understanding of morality
- An overzealous preoccupation with praise and worship
- A false and narrow view of patriotism
- An unbalanced focus on prosperity and personal enrichment themes.

McMickle further asserts that prophetic preaching happens when the preacher has the courage to speak truth to power not only inside the church building, but also in the streets, boardrooms and jail cells of the secular world, thus, the need for prophetic preaching today.

2. THE ROOTS OF RESISTANCE: MARTIN LUTHER KING, JR'S SPIRITUAL, SOCIAL AND INTELLECTUAL DEVELOPMENT

In order to comprehensively understand Dr. Martin Luther King, Jr.'s public achievement - it is critical to consider the spiritual, social and intellectual influences on his life. Throughout his public life, King consistently reached down into the deep streams of the religious experience and social integration that had been so integral to his early formation. It was within these streams that he consistently discovered and re-discovered the essence of faithfulness in God, which would ultimately sustain him in his constant beckoning for persons in the church and society to heed the words of the prophet Micah, to:

> "love kindness, and to do justice, and to walk humbly with God"
>
> (Micah 6:8) and,

The prophet Amos, to:

> "Let justice roll down as waters, and righteousness as an ever-flowing stream." (Amos 5:24)

In many of the biographical works that have been written on King, a great deal of attention has been given to his intellectual development at Morehouse College in Atlanta, Crozier Theological Seminary in Chester, Pennsylvania and Boston University where he completed his doctoral studies in 1955. Certainly, his intellectual development at these institutions, along with additional academic work at Harvard University and the University of Pennsylvania, would provide the intellectual foundation for his public ministry. These institutions would provide the "fertile ground" necessary for progress in what King would refer to as "a serious intellectual quest for a method to eliminate social evil."

But in order to fully comprehend King's movement toward a theological praxis of non-violent social resistance and direct action as a prophetic preacher and public theologian, his experiences and development in these institutions should be considered against the backdrop, and within the context of his earlier development.

There were three major influences present in King's early life that shaped his later attitudes and actions. These were:

(1) His black middle class family (which included his extended family and the family/community ethos in which he was raised)
(2) The religion of the Black Baptist church, and
(3) The patterns of racial segregation and discrimination in the South, some of which he experienced.

Lewis V. Baldwin in *There is a Balm,* suggests that King's cultural roots were "folk, black, and southern." These cultural roots remained a part of King's thought and praxis into his adult years.

Foundational to his early development were King's early family experiences. In *Liberating Visions,* Robert Franklin suggests that King's fundamental character was shaped and nurtured within the valuing context of the southern middle-class family structure. The Kings and Williamses were prominent leaders in the "new South." His family tree included a long line of Baptist preachers (his father, grandfather and great-grandfather were ministers), and outspoken advocates for freedom and justice. (Franklin 1990, 105)

King's views on racism in America can be clearly traced to his early development. In his biography, *Let the Trumpet Sound,* Stephen B. Oates reports on King's preschool years, when his closest playmate was a white boy whose father owned the store across the street from the King family home. When the two friends entered school in 1935, they attended separate schools. One day, the parents of his friend announced that M.L. could no longer play with their son. Their explanation was, "Because we are white and you are colored." (Oates 1982, 10)

Later, around the dinner table, King's parents responded to his hurt by telling him the story of the black experience in America. Oates points out that it was typically through conversations such as this (around the dinner table) that black youth would be socialized into the protest traditions of the black community and church.

King's early childhood experiences with racism predisposed him to study and address the psychological and social effects of oppression. His later formal education was predicated upon and guided by the more informal learning and personal experiences of his early years within the nurturing context of a close-knit family, church and community.

These early influences are evident in the King's later intellectual attraction to:

(1) A model of the rational, black minister as organic intellectual as modeled by Benjamin E. Mays at Morehouse College, and Mordecai Johnson at Howard University
(2) The model and method of nonviolent social transformation of Mohandas Gandhi, the Indian political/social reformer
(3) The philosophy of Personalism of Harold DeWolf and Edgar Brightman at Boston University
(4) The Dialectical Method of Georg Wilhelm Friedrich Hegel
(5) The Christian Liberalism and Social Gospel of Walter Rauschenbusch, and
(6) The Christian Realism of Reinhold Niebuhr.

And so, within the context of these cultural and intellectual influences, theologian James Cone writes of the impact of Martin Luther King's prophetic witness:

> As a prophet, with a charisma never before witnessed in this century, King preached black liberation in the light of Jesus Christ and thus aroused the spirit of

> freedom in the black community. To be sure, one may argue that his method of nonviolence did not meet the needs of the black community in an age of black power; but it is beyond question that it was King's influence and leadership in the black community which brought us to the period in which we now live, and for that we are in debt. His life and message demonstrate that the "soul" of the black community is inseparable from liberation, but always liberation grounded in Jesus Christ... (Cone 1986, 37)

The recurring theme and consistent overarching prophetic concern in King's sermons throughout his career was what he called *Beloved Community*. It was rooted in the biblical notion of *Agape* (God's unconditional love), and was the ultimate goal for which he worked.

In King's conception of *Beloved Community*, faith and action were interrelated. In this regard, King viewed theology and ethics as indelibly interconnected. Theology – what we believe and comprehend about God (how we talk about God) - could not be separated from ethics - who we are, and what we do as the human family. Our creed and our deed had to be in concert. Our talk and our walk needed to correspond.

This faith-action (creed-deed) dialectic found its ultimate expression in the notion of *Beloved Community*. For King, the vision of *Beloved Community* was of an integrated community in which persons of all races and creeds could live together harmoniously as sisters and brothers in peace. It was the Kin-dom of God on earth. King stated, "I do not think of political power as an end. Neither do I think of economic power as an end. They are ingredients in the objective we seek in life. And I think that end, that objective, is a truly brotherly society, the creation of *Beloved Community*." (King *1963*)

3. THE LEGACY OF DR. KING – WHAT MIGHT WE APPROPRIATE?

Rev. Dr. Martin Luther King, Jr. spoke to the divine and moral imperative that the church and society share in seeking to eradicate racial hatred, economic oppression and social disintegration, and advanced the appropriation of the Christian love-ethic as foundational for constructively moving toward the realization of authentic community – *Beloved Community*. King asserted that God's intent is for the human family to live in community as interrelated members. In the final analysis, King's prophetic preaching and praxis offer insight for the contemporary church and preachers - and has implications and application in at least four principle areas: *Call, Conviction, Courage and Commitment.*

Call

Over the course of King's thirteen year public ministry, it became clear that his praxis of ministry in the public sphere was ultimately rooted in a deep sense of a call by God. This sense of calling is what ultimately spawned his action. For instance, there is no indication that King had any personal intent, ambition or vocational/professional inclination to become the leader of the movement for racial and social justice in the South while in seminary or graduate school, but with the course and convergence of events within the context of his pastoral ministry at Dexter Avenue Baptist Church in Montgomery, Alabama - like Biblical prophets - King came to the conclusion that it was indeed a part of his vocation and calling to become one of the prophetic public voices of the Civil Rights movement, first in Alabama, and then beyond. Likewise, it is incumbent upon preachers today to clearly discern as to if and how they may be called by God to engage in public ministry and address prophetic concerns as they emerge.

Conviction

For King, his sense of calling was acted upon within the context of his convictions. King's convictions were largely rooted in his understanding of God and people. King believed that all persons were created by God with inherent worth, and that all people were therefore privy to the moral prerogative of human dignity and social justice. King consistently affirmed what he deemed to be the "Somebodyness" of all people regardless of race, class or other categories. (see Baker-Fletcher)

Ultimately, it was these convictions that led to his prophetic witness. Likewise, it is incumbent upon preachers who might engage in the public square today to be equally as clear about their convictions, and what they we believe about God, God's people and God's will for peace with justice.

Courage

Courage serves as the measure of the human will to act on our call and convictions – and to say and do what we believe to be just and right. Interestingly - among the books that Dr. Martin Luther King, Jr. carried with him as he travelled and provided leadership to the Civil Rights movement was Paul Tillich's *The Courage to Be.* Concerning courage, Tillich wrote, "Few constructs are as useful for analysis of the human situation. Courage is an ethical reality, but it is rooted in the whole breadth of human existence and ultimately in the structure of being itself. It must be considered ontologically in order to be understood ethically." (Tillich 1952, 1) Courage to act on one's call and convictions means one is willing to risk much of oneself - one's popularity, promotion and associations for the sake of the causes to which one feels called and convicted to prophetically address.

Commitment

In the midst of the 381 day Montgomery Bus Boycott in 1955-56, King made a statement that would become a signature of his prophetic witness when he said that "True peace in not merely the absence of tension, it is the presence of justice." He would later state that "The arc of the moral universe is long, but it bends toward justice." These two statements speak clearly to King's commitments to promote racial equality and social justice, his strivings to help eradicate what he deemed to be the "triplets of evil" - racism, poverty and war - and to help move the church and society toward becoming *Beloved Community*. It was out of his sense of calling, conviction and courage that his commitments to do justice derived. Today, prophetic preaching and praxis likewise call for clear and consistent commitment in light of calling and conviction to do justice, and the courage that we can muster to carry this out.

-31-

TEN WAYS TO BUILD THE BELOVED COMMUNITY

(This article was published in Leading Ideas by the Lewis Center for Church Leadership in January 2017.)

A universal human striving is for authentic community. Rev. Dr. Martin Luther King, Jr. was among those who framed the conception of community in what he termed the *Beloved Community.* King asserted that "all life is interrelated." This interrelatedness was rooted, for King, in the fundamental belief in the kinship of all persons. He believed that all life is part of a single process; all persons are sisters and brothers, and that we all have a place in the *Beloved Community.* Because all of us are interrelated, one cannot harm another without harming oneself.

King also said "everyone can be great because everyone could serve." In these uncertain times, churches and our broader society must make a sincere commitment to engaging in acts of compassion and justice as means of living out our faith, and loving our neighbors. Individuals, churches, groups, organizations, institutions and even governments can continue to pursue Dr. King's vision of the *Beloved Community* by making commitments to community-building and social engagement. Here are ten ways that individuals, churches, and other organizations can promote peace with justice, and build *Beloved Community.*

1. Support and develop community-wide plans aimed at expanding economic opportunities for racial-ethnic persons and women specifically in the areas of housing, banking and employment practices.

2. Actively participate in programs that reach out to help those in the most need – the hungry, the homeless and the unemployed.

3. Do your part to assure that every inner city and rural young person can look forward to an adequate education. Adopt an inner-city or rural school. Offer your skills where appropriate.

4. Encourage schools, colleges and universities in your area to include the teachings of Dr. King and other freedom fighters in their curricula and programs.

5. Take specific actions to deal with the problems of drugs, alcohol dependency, teenage pregnancy and family violence in your community.

6. Advocate for the removal of all weapons from our streets, homes and schools. Support causes that promote freedom, justice and peace abroad.

7. Help extend human rights, dignity, health and economic well-being to all persons.

8. Actively oppose groups that promote hatred and violence. Vigilantly oppose racism, homophobia,

xenophobia and other forms of hatred in our communities.

9. Sponsor and participate in programs that encourage interracial, intercultural and inter-religious goodwill and unity.

10. Read the Social Principles of your denomination or faith tradition, and strive to make them an integral part of your life and the life of your religious community and social circles.

-32-

WHEN ENOUGH IS ENOUGH

(This commentary was published in the United Methodist Connection of the Baltimore-Washington Conference of the United Methodist Church on Friday, July 8, 2016 in the aftermath of the police-involved deaths of Alton Sterling (Baton Rouge, LA) and Philando Castile (Minneapolis, MN), and the shooting deaths of five police officers in Dallas, TX.)

About this week, first, I believe we all need to be in prayer for the families of those five police officers who were shot and lost their lives in Dallas, TX last night. Of course, Blue Lives Matter, as do all lives, but what has gotten us to the place where we are as a nation, going back to before the death of Trayvon Martin in Sanford, Florida in February 2012 is whether - based on ongoing instances of police brutality against Black people and an unwillingness/inability of the nation's criminal justice system - in a number of cases - to hold anybody accountable for such police brutality - we as a nation really believe that Black Lives Matter.

This is not a matter of either/or, but yes/and. In light of this, I see the protests and outrage following the police-involved killings of Alton Sterling in Baton Rouge, LA and Philando Castile in Minneapolis, MN earlier this week as being justified. I agree with Dr. Martin Luther King, Jr. who intimated that riots are the language of the unheard. The people involved in peaceful protest across the nation are choosing to act out and speak out on some things that have been brought to light this week because of video, but these incidents of police brutality are occurring every day in communities across the nation, and many people feel that they are unheard in the midst of it all.

On average, three people have died at the hands of police every day since Michael Brown was killed by a police office in Ferguson, MO in August 2014. Most of these deaths are never brought to light in national media, but the people who are affected know that they have occurred and they continue to hurt because of the lack of justice in too many of these cases, and because of a sense that Black people are being dehumanized, and that Black lives don't really matter – or matter less than other lives - in the eyes of too many people. Those who have died are sons and daughters, sisters and brothers, fathers and mothers - as were Sterling and Castile. They have names as did Sterling and Castile.

As for the action that must follow the peaceful protests and outrage, this is a matter of sustained, concerted commitment, and most importantly it is a matter of leadership. Leaders, whoever and wherever they are, must get beyond institutional and political posturing and (in the case of church leadership) denominational turf and maintenance insularity and fear, and move into risk-taking witness and leadership that mobilizes people and moves them into action that starts to make demands for systemic change. The time has come for religious leaders from all denominations and religious persuasions – from the left, right and middle, and for espoused community organizers/activists/leaders and politicians everywhere in the nation to speak with clear prophetic voices about the nation's (church's and society's) divine imperative, moral prerogative, and plan to move above and beyond the moral muck and mire in which we now find ourselves.

-33-

TEN WAYS TO STRENGTHEN CHURCH, COMMUINITY AND POLICE RELATIONS

(This article was published in Leading Ideas by the Lewis Center for Church Leadership in March 2017.)

One key to a church's vitality is the quality of the relationships it establishes with a broad spectrum of leaders and institutions throughout its community. One of the most important set of relationships a church can develop is with police and other public safety officials. Recent well-publicized police-involved shootings and deaths, and the shootings and deaths of a number of police officers around the nation have stained police-community relations and resulted in unrest in many communities.

Working proactively rather than reactively to strengthen a church's relationships with its surrounding community and with police and other public safety officials engenders trust. These strengthened relationships also help improve the quality of life for persons living and working in particular communities. It is a part of the theological task of churches to "seek the welfare" (shalom, peace, well-being) of all people in their respective communities (Jeremiah 29:7). Individuals, churches, groups, organizations, institutions, and even government entities can promote the well-being of communities by making a sincere commitment to strengthening the relationship between the church, the community and the police.

Here are ten ways that individuals, churches, and other community organizations can work toward strengthening these relationships.

1. Pray for the police serving your community.

2. Pray for and publically affirm the police and other public safety officials who are members of your congregation.

3. Know your community police officers by name, and keep their contact information readily available. Schedule regular meetings with community police officers to establish and strengthen relationships.

4. Participate in periodic ride-alongs and community walks with police and community leaders.

5. Invite police to community events held by the church, such as back-to-school events, community meals, and food giveaways.

6. Include local police on the distribution lists for the church newsletter and email communications.

7. Seek to collaborate with community entities like the Chambers of Commerce, NAACP, community associations, PTAs, other churches in the community across denominations, and other faith traditions to address common interests and concerns regarding policing and public safety.

8. Invite community police to speak to youth and young adults in the church.

9. Educate youth and adults on appropriate conduct if stopped by police.

10. Assist police departments in the recruitment of qualified persons in the congregation and community who would serve well as uniformed police officers, especially women and minorities who may be underrepresented.

-34-

GOD'S GOT A BONE T0 PICK WITH US

(This sermon was first preached at Ames Memorial United Methodist Church in Baltimore, Maryland in January 2014.)

The hand of the LORD was on me, and he brought me out by the Spirit of the LORD and set me in the middle of a valley; it was full of bones. He led me back and forth among them, and I saw a great many bones on the floor of the valley, bones that were very dry. He asked me, "Son of man, can these bones live?" I said, "Sovereign LORD, you alone know." Then he said to me, "Prophesy to these bones and say to them, 'Dry bones, hear the word of the LORD! This is what the Sovereign LORD says to these bones: I will make breath enter you, and you will come to life. I will attach tendons to you and make flesh come upon you and cover you with skin; I will put breath in you, and you will come to life. Then you will know that I am the LORD.'" So I prophesied as I was commanded. And as I was prophesying, there was a noise, a rattling sound, and the bones came together, bone to bone. I looked, and tendons and flesh appeared on them and skin covered them, but there was no breath in them. Then he said to me, "Prophesy to the breath; prophesy, son of man, and say to it, 'This is what the Sovereign LORD says: Come, breath, from the four winds and breathe into these slain, that they may live.'" So I prophesied as he commanded me, and

breath entered them; they came to life and stood up on their feet—a vast army. (Ezekiel 37:1-10)

Any careful look at our world today makes it clear that there's trouble in the land. All around us, we see evidence of societal decline and moral decay. Crime and drugs permeate too many of our communities. The economy continues to suffer as the rich among us get richer, and too many of the rest of us merely get by. Hatred and separation remind us of the work that we have before us in reconciling with God and with one another.

It was the great German philosopher Friedrich Nietzsche who reminded the world after the French Revolution that the absence in our world of much that really makes any sense among us leads many people to question the very existence of God. Indeed, what we are left with is an apparent "nihilism" – a certain nothingness, a certain meaninglessness, a certain lovelessness, a certain hopelessness – indeed a certain crisis of hope.

The conditions of our world today are similar to those which the prophet Ezekiel had to address in his day. Some 2700 years ago, Ezekiel was called to address the national problems of Judea. The nation had been utterly vanquished in war, and the temple was in ruins. The people had lost virtually all hope that their future would be any better than their present.

And Ezekiel offers the people a picture – a vivid description of what he sees. He says that he had been placed down in a valley. And in the valley, Ezekiel encountered the predicament of dry bones – where there was no life, no movement, and no being. All that he saw were dry bones.

This passage from Ezekiel 37 is always a fascinating narrative, for I believe it speaks to all of the very real human conditions of brokenness, despair and "dryness" that God's people – you and I - face in any given day and age.

Certainly, this matter of dry bones is a universal predicament, and the story is relevant – we can relate to Ezekiel – because life has set all of us down in the midst of some dry bones at one time or another.

Indeed, in life we often find ourselves in situations so barren, so difficult, and apparently so hopeless that we are not sure if we will ever see our way out.

And so when we read of what Ezekiel describes as the valley of dry bones, we should recognize the landscape. We've all put in some time in that valley.

When a loved one dies… after a marriage or other relationship breaks down… when depression sets in like a heavy, wet, smothering blanket… when material resources are limited, and may dry up (and the bills have to get paid)… when your faith is weak… when your mind and emotions are confused… after a failure – when stinging humiliation seems to tear flesh off the bones… when illness has struck… and when death has descended into our lives. Dry bones have been in the midst of each and every one of our lives.

Ezekiel looked around and all he saw were dry bones in his midst. And furthermore, he likened the spiritual condition of Israel to dry bones. What was Ezekiel talking about? We know that that which is dry is that which is without moisture. It is that which is dry lacks fluidity. When something becomes dry it lacks life.

And the truth of the matter is that the people had brought a lot of their spiritual dryness on themselves, and God had a controversy with the way the people were living. The people had been killed off – life had been taken out of the land – because they had forgotten how to follow the Lord who had been their God, and who had delivered them in the past. God had a bone to pick with them.

And I want to suggest that God also had a bone to pick with us today. In the midst of the trouble in the land, we need to look ourselves in our spiritual mirror, and ask ourselves the question – how have we as a nation, and how have we even as the church turned our face away from God? And what role do we really have to play in the trouble in our midst today? Could it be that God's got a bone to pick with us?

All Ezekiel saw in the land were dry bones. And in the midst of this, God asked Ezekiel this haunting question: "Can these dry bones live?"

And as a remedy, God said to Ezekiel, "I want you to go down into the valley and prophesy (speak) to the dry bones." Strange instructions these were, "Go down there Ezekiel, and start working with what you have, and start speaking possibility and hope directly into the hopelessness in your midst. It does not matter that there appears to be no hope or life, (God said) just start speaking my promise and my hope into the dry bones, and let my Spirit do the rest."

Indeed, strange instructions they were, but we need to realize that sometimes God calls us to radical, unorthodox, "crazy" faithfulness. Sometimes God uses strange tactics for God's glory to be revealed, and for God to get glory out of our lives. God told Ezekiel to do a radical thing, and "Prophesy to the dry bones, and watch me bring hope and life to my people." God's ways are not our ways and God's thoughts are not ours!

And as Ezekiel spoke to the dry bones, all he had to do was then watch God work. The word tells us that God took the bones, and God connected the ligaments and the tendons and the cartilage, and God connected the nerves and put blood into the dry bodies. The bones received sinew and flesh, and after a while, breath and life came into those bones, and they stood on their feet and began to move.

The word of hope today is that we know that dry bones can indeed live. Whatever they look like in your life – dry bones can live. We know that the same God who brought Ezekiel's people from despair to hope… the same God who brought hope to a defeated nation… the same God who raised Jesus from the dead… the same God who delivered people through the Middle Passage and the Holocaust… the same God who has made a way out of no way for others… is present in the world today, and will be tomorrow, and God can and will revive the dry bones in our midst!

-35-
DREAMS AND NIGHTMARES: REFLECTIONS ON THE 2016 PRESIDENTIAL ELECTION

(This article was originally posted on my blog at www.newurbanminstryblogspot.com in the aftermath of the U.S. Presidential election in November 2016.)

The election of Donald Trump as the 45th President of the United States on November 9, 2016 should not have been a surprise to anybody who had been paying attention to the racial/social/political climate in the nation over the last 16 years. The writing began to be most clearly scrolled on the nation's wall in 2008 with the rise of Sarah Palin (prior to President Barack Obama's election in November 2008), the rise of right-wing Tea Party politics, the rise of the "Birther" movement, with the preponderance of ultra-obstructionist governance in both houses of the United States Congress, and the alarming rise of militias and hate groups across the nation.

The fissures in the social fabric of the nation really began to be evident with the politics of race and class so prevalent during the presidential tenure of George W. Bush (2000-2008). The truth is that racism is and has been, since the nation's founding, the elephant in the nation's living room – what Rev. Jim Wallis refers to as America's original sin. The 2016 presidential race and the election of Trump merely served to confirm that America is what many people already knew it is, and bring to light for some others what they have just been in denial about.

In the 2016 election's aftermath, many Americans who have felt the inordinate scourge of racism, sexism, classism and various forms of xenophobia – and yet still have held out hope that the United States would become an authentically inclusive, post-racial, post-racist nation – now should understand more fully what Dr. Martin Luther King, Jr. meant when he intimated on May 8, 1967, less than four years after his famous "I Have a Dream" speech in August 1963 in the Nation's Capital and less than a year before his assassination, that his dream for America had in large measure become a nightmare. King stated, "I must confess that that dream that I had... has at many points become a nightmare. Now I'm not one to lose hope, I keep on hoping, I still have faith in the future... but I've come to see that we have many more difficult days ahead, and some of the old optimism was a little superficial, and now it must be tempered with a solid realism. The realistic fact is we have a long, long way to go."

I resonate with Dr. King's sentiments. I was born in a Freedman's Bureau hospital in Washington, DC, the nation's capital at a time when the federal city was largely racially segregated. I went to segregated inner city public schools and lived in segregated communities for the first 15 years on my life. Growing up, although we were told we could be anything we wanted to be, I never really dreamed that I'd live to see a president who looked anything like me.

I'm reflecting on the fact that with the election of Donald Trump, the nation elected as its 45th president the person who, by being the very face and voice of the Birther movement, effectively sought - and in no small way served - to delegitimize the presidency of Barack H. Obama, the 44th president, and first African American to serve as president of the United States.

This is why some of us will find it difficult, if not impossible, to reconcile this, to square in our minds and hearts that Trump will now serve as president of the United States. The effort to delegitimize the citizenship, and thus the presidency, of President Obama - born in this same nation as me - was effectively an effort to delegitimize me, my sons, daughter, nephews, nieces, wife, father, mother, brothers, sisters and every person who looks like us, and - like us - were born on this hallowed soil - girls and boys who have now indeed seen a president who looks like them, and so they now can dream, likewise, to be president someday.

For many non-Whites, the race problem in America is viewed through the lenses of the election results and the hate-related violence that has ensued. It is further exacerbated by the religious conundrum found with the fact that white evangelical Christians and Catholics voted overwhelmingly to elect Trump as president, and are largely responsible for his victory. Post-election data shows that at least 81 percent of white evangelical Christians across denominations voted for Trump. These statistics include many upper middle class and wealthy suburban whites who identify as being members of mainline Christian denominations - and who may not openly identify as evangelicals by denomination – but who voted for Trump in significant numbers. Many of these persons indicated that they based their voting decisions primarily on the "morality only" argument - and the notion that Trump would align his political agenda as president with evangelical and Catholic values on issues like abortion, the selection of the next Supreme Court Justice(s), same sex marriage, and transgender accommodations in public facilities.

The focus on "morality only" as the primary reason why so many white Christians voted for Trump is simplistic, and might very well be a misguided assumption at best, and disingenuous at worst. This argument does not give credence to some other clear reasons why persons voted for Trump. It does not give credence to the race/ethnicity dynamic – Trump's stated agenda that would adversely affect many Latina/os, Muslims and Blacks in various ways. Nor does it give credence to the division and fear of the "other" that Trump tapped into during his campaign for president among whites across socio-economic lines. Furthermore, it does not give credence to the acts of hatred among many whites toward Obama, regardless of what he did as president, and by extension hatred of Hillary Clinton, and by further extension their hatred of Black and Brown people (that is in a nutshell the essence of racism).

It does not give credence to the fact that the economy is much improved under Obama's leadership over in the last 8 years (with lower unemployment, lower interest rates, lower foreclosure rates, and a rising stock market). It does not take into account that whatever their rationale, persons voted to elect a person, in Trump, who demonstrated behaviors before and during his campaign for president that pointed to the very real prospect that he is emotionally, psychologically and temperamentally unfit to lead the nation, and - by Christian standards – engages in various behaviors that would be considered to be immoral (sexism, misogyny, racism, classism, economic exploitation and xenophobia).

After the election, many poor, blue collar, working class white Americans have said that they voted for Trump based on his vague, non-specific promises of improving economic opportunities for them. In-fact, based on history and data, these persons voted against their economic best-interests. For instance, based on prognosticators' analysis of the first tax cut proposed by the President-elect's camp and the Republican-led Congress in the week following the election, approximately 47% of that tax cut would benefit the richest 1% of the population.

The fact is that supply-side, trickle down approaches to stimulating the economy - invariably pushed by the Republican party - never have and never will work to improve the overall economic plight of poor and working class Americans, barring an economic miracle of tsunamic proportions.

This proved to be the case with the failed supply-side policies of Ronald Reagan, George H.W. Bush and George W. Bush. Supply-side economics has in the past, and will more than likely in the future result in higher inflation, slower than normal job growth, higher interest rates, more de-regulation and slower than normal growth in the Gross Domestic Product, while the richest segment of the population will invariably benefit from such approaches through expanded wealth accumulation. The bottom line is that the rich tend to operate first and foremost from their logical self-interests of wealth accumulation and not from the interest of the common good and the redistribution of wealth across the economy through job creation and increasing wages.

Poverty and suffering are no respecters of skin color, race, neighborhood or geography (rural or urban). Across race and ethnicity, poor and working class persons are likely to suffer disproportionately with the nation's choice of the next president. The nation may well discover that for those who are now in control at the highest levels of national government. Trump's presidential campaign was not fundamentally about ending abortion or same-sex marriage, or even about expanding in any pronounced way, the Second Amendment rights to bear arms - it was about enacting economic policies that are most likely to benefit the wealthiest Americans at the expense of the further marginalization of those who have the least among us.

What is clear is that America is a nation that is deeply divided, and this did not begin, nor will it change, with the election results. We were deeply divided before the election and the same is true afterwards. And there are really no winners in a fight as deeply divisive as the one we've experienced with this election cycle. All of us in some way have lost, which would have been the case even if the election results had turned out differently.

It's a dark night in the nation, but it's important not to forget that before the election and in the days after it, many people of all hues have known, and will continue to know, of dark nights personally. Most of those who were homeless before the election are still homeless, the hungry are still hungry, the hurting still hurt, and the imprisoned are still imprisoned.

But as always, there is hope. The nation can yet realize the words etched in our Declaration of Independence – "We hold these truths to be self-evident that all (people) are created equal", and can come to realize in no insignificant way the Latin words imbedded in our nation's credo – *e pluribus unum* – "out of many one."

The nation can heal from our now deeply open wounds of racism, sexism, classic, militarism and incivility - but it won't be easy, and it's not in any way a certainty. As people of faith, the best we can do is heed the words of Solomon to a people in national distress and turmoil in another age, *"If my people who are called by my name, will humble themselves and pray, and seek my face, and turn from their wicked ways, I will hear their cries, and I will heal the land."* (2 Chronicles 7:14)

Dr. Martin Luther King, Jr. intimated that "the arc of the moral universe is long, but it bends towards justice." It is important to realize that this arc won't bend on its own. It will take the providence of God almighty and the tenacious, courageous efforts and actions of people of conscience and good will who are willing to work for justice and equality, peace and unity in the days ahead. May it be so.

-36-

A WAKE-UP CALL

(This sermon was preached on Sunday, November 13, 2016, the Sunday after the 2016 U.S. presidential election at Epworth Chapel United Methodist Church, Baltimore, MD.)

To the angel of the church in Sardis write: These are the words of him who holds the seven sprits of God and the seven stars. I know your deeds; you have a reputation of being alive, but you are dead. Wake up! Strengthen what remains and is about to die, for I have found your deeds unfinished in the sight of my God. Remember, therefore, what you have received and heard; hold it fast, and repent. But if you do not wake up, I will come like a thief, and you will not know at what time I will come to you. Yet you have a few people in Sardis who have not soiled their clothes. They will walk with me, dressed in white, for they are worthy. (Revelation 3:1-4)

Eight years ago, almost to this day, I can recall the great joy and euphoria that many of us felt with the election of Barack Hussein Obama as the 44th President of the United States. I recall election night and watching with amazement as the crowds gathered at around midnight in Grant Park in the center of Chicago to celebrate President Obama's election.

I remember – as I'm sure many of us do – the Presidential Inauguration in January 2009 in Washington,

DC, the city where I was born and raised, and the pride that we shared in the historic election of the first African-American president of these United States. This pride that swelled in many of us was married with great hope and expectation that we, as a nation, had come to the place where we could finally realize in no small way what the words in our nation's Declaration of Independence really mean – "We hold these truths to be self-evident that all (people) are created equal" – and that we had come to realize in no insignificant way the Latin words imbedded in our nation's credo – *e pluribus unum* – out of many one.

As we fast forward eight years, we now find ourselves at the dawning of a very new, difficult and troubling reality. And this is not merely because of the fact that the nation has elected as its 45th president a person who has largely expressed disdain and derision toward the interests of immigrants, Muslims, many Latina/os and Black persons, women, the disabled, and city dwellers in this nation. But we find ourselves at the dawning of this very different day, confronted by a new and difficult reality because in many ways the hopes and dreams that many of us shared in 2008 have been delayed, if not denied. In many ways – as Dr. Martin Luther King, Jr. intimated in May 1967 – less than four years after his marvelous and prophetic "I Have a Dream" speech in August 1963 - his dream had in very real ways turned into a nightmare.

And if the truth is told, we find ourselves at the dawning of this very different, and for many of us a troubling, reality – a very dark night in the nation - because we as a society and indeed as the church have slept on our opportunities.

Like Rip van Winkle – the fictional character in the story set around the time of the Revolutionary War - we have been in a prolonged slumber – snoozing away opportunity after opportunity to improve our lives, to improve our family life, to make things better for our children, to build our communities, to make our cities better, to make our schools better, to invest our resources, to advocate for those who have the least and are the lost and left out among us, and to even grow and vitalize our churches.

We've been asleep, snoozing away our future and that of our children. We have been on prolonged snooze control – hearing the alarm bells – but in no small ways ignoring them over and over again.

And so, this election and where we now find ourselves as a people, as a nation, and as the church has to be for us a wakeup call. If we look at Scripture, we find that we are not the first people who have needed to wake up. All we need to do this morning is have a talk with the church in Sardis to find out that this is not the first time that God's people have gone to sleep.

So let's call up Sardis to see what we can learn from them. If we talk to the people of Sardis, we find out that Sardis is one of seven churches that God dealt with in the Book of Revelation. God had problems with all seven of the churches in Revelation, but God's specific problem with the church at Sardis was that they had fallen asleep and needed to wake up.

So God sent John of Patmos to remind Sardis of what they had once been. They had once been a vital, vibrant, caring, compassionate, committed community of faith. They had hope and they lived in that hope. They had worked to make things better. They had loved one another, done justice, and walked humbly with God.

Sardis didn't blame their problems on the government or who was president or not. They prayed and they came to church. They held each other accountable. They trusted God and believed that in their faithfulness, God would make things better for their children and grandchildren than it was for them.

If we were to talk to Sardis this morning, they would tell us that they then became complacent and comfortable in their blessings. They had education and jobs and some money and homes and cars and pension plans. So they felt like they didn't need to work as hard, pray as hard, or worship as much. The church at Sardis had a reputation, but they had lost their sense of responsibility. They had a remnant of religion, but had lost a sense of what it meant to be in relationship with God.

And they started to see all their hopes and dreams begin to be trumped.

And God's word through John of Patmos was simply that all Sardis needed to do was *wake up* - that where they found themselves was just being at the point of a *wake-up call*... and that if and when they woke up, God would bless them again as God had done before.

All this is for you and me is a wake-up call. The trials and trouble that we find ourselves in the midst of today is a wake-up call. This pain and disappointment – and yes for some of us anger and fear – which we now experience, is a wake-up call – a call to turn back to God, and watch God begin to make things right for us again.

It's a wake-up call to put our faith, trust, hopes and dreams in nobody and nothing but Jesus. Indeed, our hopes and dreams don't really rest with who's in the White House or not – not with Barack Obama, Hillary Clinton, Bernie Sanders or Donald Trump. Our hope is in Jesus. Our hope is not in how high the eagle flies, but in the power of Jesus, our Lord.

So keep holding onto your hopes and dreams. Keep standing on the promises and possibilities that we see in God. In the midst of this - heed the words of the great poet – Langston Hughes – "Hold fast to dreams – for when dreams die – life is a broken winged bird that cannot fly." ("Dreams")

As the Song-writer wrote – "(Our) hope is built on nothing less, than Jesus' blood and righteousness. (We) dare not trust the sweetest frame, but wholly lean on Jesus' name. On Christ, the solid rock (we) stand. All other ground is sinking sand!" ("My Hope is Built")

-37-

LESSONS FOR A LUKEWARM CHURCH

(This sermon was preached on Sunday, November 20 2016, two Sundays after the 2016 presidential election at Epworth Chapel United Methodist Church, Baltimore, MD.)

"To the angel of the church in Laodicea write: These are the words of the Amen, the faithful and true witness, the ruler of God's creation. I know your deeds, that you are neither cold nor hot. I wish you were either one or the other! So, because you are lukewarm—neither hot nor cold—I am about to spit you out of my mouth. You say, 'I am rich; I have acquired wealth and do not need a thing.' But you do not realize that you are wretched, pitiful, poor, blind and naked. I counsel you to buy from me gold refined in the fire, so you can become rich; and white clothes to wear, so you can cover your shameful nakedness; and salve to put on your eyes, so you can see. (Revelation 3:14-18)

These last two weeks have found many people in the midst of heated conversation. Anywhere you find news on the television, on newsstands, or on the Internet - there seems to be heated conversation about the past presidential election.

The heated discussions have extended into the church, where it's clear that even Christians, those of us who profess to be followers of Jesus, are not of the same mind about the implications of the presidential election on the well-being of all God's people.

Indeed, many people are passionate in their beliefs about the efficacy, or not, of the election. And if the truth is told, this has resulted in often heated conversations, even among Christians.

It leads us to wonder, what if the church and society were as passionate about other important things as we are about who the President-elect is, who will be on his cabinet and how he will govern after the Presidential Inauguration? What if we were as passionate about doing good, doing no harm and staying in love with God?

What if the whole church and society were as passionate about feeding the hungry, clothing the naked, and housing the homeless? What if we were as passionate about seeking peace with justice in the world, and working for peace on the streets of Baltimore and other cities?

What if we were as passionate about ensuring that every child got a great education, that police brutality came to an end, and that more good jobs were available for more people?

The truth of the matter is that when it comes to many of the things that really matter to people – if our temperature was taken this morning, we would be neither hot or cold. We would be lukewarm. Indeed, our witness in the world for the sake of Jesus would be measured as lackluster, lackadaisical and lukewarm.

And we are not the first church to find ourselves in the predicament of being lackluster and lukewarm. If we took a few minutes to have a conversation with the church at Laodicea, we would find out that they were in a similar place.

If we were to talk to those in Laodicea this morning, they'd tell us that they were at one point a vital, vibrant community of faith. They would tell us that they, at one point, were on fire for Jesus – they prayed without ceasing, they worshipped with vigor, they helped the hurting and helpless around them, they did justice, loved kindness and walked in humility with God.

But then they'd tell us that at some point, they came to a place where their Holy Ghost fire left them. They got tired and stale in their witness. They were getting by - week after week, Sunday after Sunday - doing just enough not to get ice cold and totally frigid, but neither were they hot. *They were lukewarm.* To quote the sentiments of the great blues singer, B. B. King, - "The thrill was gone" for them.

Those in Laodicea found themselves being both in the world and of the world. They were religious, but not in relationship with Jesus. It was difficult to tell the church in Laodicea from the world around them. And so it had gotten to the point that because the church didn't seem to stand for much of anything anymore, the people in the world didn't feel they needed the church or God in their lives. The church was lukewarm.

The church in Laodicea had become a *thermometer* that reflected the temperature of the world, instead of being a *thermostat* that set the temperature and the atmosphere for the world. And because they didn't stand for much of anything, they began to fall for almost everything.

Then the church at Laodicea would tell you and me that God sent John of Patmos by their city to let them know that God was not pleased with the fact that they were doing just enough to get by. And John told them that God was so concerned with their lukewarm-ness, that God no longer wanted anything to do with them.

The lesson here is that these are times for deep introspection and soul-searching for the church – for you and me. Everything we're going through right now affords you and me an opportunity to first look within ourselves – to examine ourselves - and then look outside among ourselves to see how we can recapture our desire to know, love and serve God.

First, we need to look within ourselves, to search our souls, to ask ourselves the questions, "Am I really seeking after God? Am I loving and serving God with my whole heart? Am I growing in my ability to love everybody – even those who might not love me back?

Then secondly, we need to look outside ourselves, and ask the questions, "Are we being the church that God calls us to be? Are we worshipping to glorify God, or is our "worship" just a show? Are we serving to help somebody, or are we more concerned about who will recognize and reward us? Are we showing and telling others about the love, grace and mercy of God in Christ?"

Are we so on fire for Jesus that other people stop us and wonder how they can catch the flame that we have, or is our fire so dull that it can barely be felt or seen?

The real lesson for a lukewarm church is that only God almighty can really light your fire. Only Jesus, the light of the world, can really light your fire.

Politicians, whoever they are, won't light it. Preachers, however well they preach won't necessarily light it. Choirs, no matter how well they sing, won't really light it. Family and friends, no matter how much they love you, can't light it.

So we need to put our faith, belief, hope and trust in God, and God alone. "*Trust in the Lord with all your heart, lean not on your own understanding, but in all your ways acknowledge God, and God will direct your path.*" (Proverbs 3:5-6)

Trust God to keep you in the midst of this. Trust God to comfort you. Trust God to provide for you. Trust God to perfect you. Trust God to make things right for you. Trust God to light the fire in you and me.

" 'Tis so sweet to trust in Jesus...
and to take him at his word...
Just to rest upon his promise...
and to know, thus saith the Lord.
Jesus, Jesus – how I trust him...
how I proved him over and over...
Jesus, Jesus precious Jesus,
O for grace to trust him more."
("'Tis So Sweet")

-38-

WHAT BECOMES OF THE BROKENHEARTED?

(This sermon was preached on Sunday, November 27 2016, three Sundays after the 2016 presidential election at Epworth Chapel United Methodist Church, Baltimore, MD.)

"My God, my God, why have you forsaken me? Why are you so far from saving me, so far from my cries of anguish? My God, I cry out by day, but you do not answer, by night, but I find no rest. Yet you are enthroned as the Holy One; you are the one Israel praises. In you our ancestors put their trust; they trusted and you delivered them. To you they cried out and were saved; in you they trusted and were not put to shame. (Psalm 22:1-5)

If I can be transparent for a few moments, there have been only a few times in my life when I have been truly brokenhearted. Among them was when our son, Marcus William Hunt died from an accidental drowning on August 7, 2005. Another was on September 11, 2001, with the terrorist attacks on the World Trade Center in New York City, in Pennsylvania and at the Pentagon in Virginia. Yet another was at the assassination of Rev. Dr. Martin Luther King, Jr. on April 4, 1968 when I was seven years old. And a fourth was at the presidential election on this November 8, 2016.

If you've ever been brokenhearted, you know what it feels like, and you can feel the same pain that I'm still experiencing in the aftermath of the past presidential election. To be clear, at its core, this is not a political concern – it is more an existential concern – getting to the very core of who I am, who we are as the people of God, and my hope for the world in which we live.

Indeed, many of us right now are living with broken spirits - broken hopes and dreams - broken hearts. It would not be an overstatement to declare that the experience of broken heartedness is often accompanied by a sense that one has been *punched in the gut* so hard, and knocked down to the point that one finds it difficult to get back up. The brokenheartedness that I'm talking about today carries with it profound disappointment, dis-heartedness, confusion, anguish and pain – and indeed fear – fear for the future of God's creation. And this brokenness often leads to bitter tears of despair – *which may seem to drip with no end in sight.*

At its core, this brokenheartedness is connected with a wonder - a question - about where God is in all that has occurred. *Is God present?* And if so, how and why would an all-powerful and all-knowing God allow that which threatens good for many of God's people in any way to occur?

This is what the psalmist in Psalm 22 was addressing. As we make our way to this song, we find ourselves parked at a *blues song.* The psalmist – who most scholars believe is

David – *is singing the blues* – and he asks God a question, *"Why Lord, have you forsaken me?* These are the very same despairing words that Jesus uttered on Calvary's cross as recorded in Matthew 27 and Mark 15, *"My God, my God, why have you forsaken me?"*

David is singing the blues. If we talked to David this morning, he'd tell us that some terrible things had gone on in his life that served to *break his heart.* Maybe it was the death of a loved one. It could have been a relationship that he thought would never end that did. It could have been something, anything that he never expected to happen, that did happen. *Why God?*

Whatever the "it" was for David, "it" served to break his heart, and led him into a deep theological, spiritual and existential conundrum. "Why, God would you allow this – (whatever *this* was) - to happen to me - a person of faith? You are the very same God who my parents put their trust in, and you blessed them, saved them - but now I am going through *this.* You are the very same God I love with my whole heart. *Why God?*"

Indeed, the theological, spiritual and existential conundrum that we find ourselves in as a nation and as the church today is a concern of theodicy - the question of the very justice and fairness of God. The fundamental question to God right now is *"Why, Lord?"* (Psalm 22)

""*"God, why?"* Why, if you are a good and loving God, would you - could you - allow bad things to happen to your people (any of your people)?"

"Why God, do you allow evil - *racism, sexism, classism, xenophobia, militarism, misogyny, homophobia, anti-Semitism, Islamophobia* - to exist and persist among us?"

God Why? Rabbi Harold Kushner posed a similar concern, with the prolonged illness of his own son, in his book, *Why Bad Things Happen to Good People.* Even for good people – faithful people, those who walk by faith and not by sight, this question of "*Why?*" is real. Why is there so much suffering in the world?

It is a perennial question. *God Why?* Somehow, for some reason - on the existential, theological and moral spectrum, God allows evil to exist in our world. God *is all-powerful and all-present*, and yet evil exists. God is *all-caring and all-knowing,* and yet we get sick… yet loved ones die... yet persons remain hungry, homeless, hurting and in need of help.

Jimmy Ruffin posed this concern about broken-heartedness in a soul song in 1966 –

(refrain) Now what becomes of the brokenhearted
Who has love that's now departed
I know I've got to find
Some kind of peace of mind -

What becomes of the brokenhearted? To answer this question, the only thing that we who walk by faith can put our trust, confidence and hope in now is the fact that just as God did not foreclose on David and the Israelites - God does not, and will not foreclose on you and me.

What becomes of the brokenhearted? In these days, we must put our faith, trust and hope even more than ever in Almighty God – and believe more than ever before that *the arc of the moral universe is long, but it (always) bends toward justice.* We must believe now more than ever before that if we do our part – if we pray without ceasing… if we love unconditionally….if we work while it's day – God will do what God has always done, and save God's people.

What becomes of the brokenhearted? I'm glad to tell you that David lived to sing something other than the blues - *and so will we.* David sang at other places -

> *"I've been young, and I've been old, but I've never seen the righteous forsaken – or his seed begging for bread."* (Psalm 37:25)

He sang -

> *"Weeping may endure for a night –*
> *but joy will come in the morning!"* (Psalm 30:5)

-39-

PRAISING THROUGH OUR PAIN

(This sermon was preached on Sunday, December 4, 2016, four Sundays after the 2016 presidential election at Epworth Chapel United Methodist Church, Baltimore, MD.)

"I will bless the LORD at all times; God's praise shall continually be in my mouth. My soul makes its boast in the LORD; let the humble hear and be glad. O magnify the LORD with me, and let us exalt his name together. (Psalm 34:1-8)

"My soul magnifies the Lord, and my spirit rejoices in God my Savior, for he has looked on the humble estate of his servant. For behold, from now on all generations will call me blessed; for he who is mighty has done great things for me, and holy is his name. (Luke1:46-48)

These are days of tremendous, and, some would suggest unprecedented transition among us. For better or for worse, we are seeing and experiencing things, which most of us would agree, we have not experienced in our lifetimes, and much of which we did not expect to experience. This transition is often seen in tragedies – both natural and human-involved - that come our way, and that have become too commonplace among us.

Bishop Yvette Flunder, in a song several years ago, sang rather prophetically about that which we experience today:

"Tragedies are commonplace...
all kinds of diseases, people are slipping away.
Economies down, people can't get enough pay....
Folks without homes, living out in the streets...
And the drug habit some say they just can't beat...
Muggers and robbers, no place seems to be safe...
("Thank You")

Indeed, tragedies are commonplace among us. And so while our attention over the past several weeks has been fixed on the national presidential campaign and presidential election - and the disappointment, anxiety, fear, and indeed trauma and drama that many people still feel and experience in light of the political quagmire that we now find ourselves in as a nation - there are transitions going on all around us.

Today, about a month after the presidential election – many people are still hurting, still unhoused and still hungry. People are still dying on many of our city's streets. Wars are still being fought in lands around the world. And some may feel hopeless and helpless in the midst of it all.

This type of transition often manifests itself in pain among us. There are consequences for all of our minds, bodies and spirits to the swift transition and tragedy that is all around us. This is to say that all of us, in some significant ways, are affected by what's happening in our world.

And so how are we to deal with transition, tragedy and pain? How might people of faith in God – those who walk by faith and not by sight - deal with all that's going on? What might our response, as God's people, be?

For some answers to these questions, we can go to Scripture and talk to King David. In our conversation with David, one of the things he would tell us this morning is that, *"I will bless the Lord at all times."*

"I will bless the Lord at all times - not sometimes… not just when I feel like it… not only when things are going my way… not only when things are working for my good… not only when things are working to my advantage in life… *but I will bless the Lord at all times."*

How could this be, that David could tell people some 3000 years ago, and tell us today, that he would bless the Lord at all times?

This was the same David who had received several threats on his life… the same David who at points in his life had to go to God in such deep despair and shame that he needed to plea for mercy… the same David who talked about going through a *"valley of the shadow of death"*.

And yet, King David says, "I'm going to bless God at all times." *In other words, I will praise God even in and through my pain.*

How could it be? It is because David knew from personal experience that whatever the situations that he found himself in over his life, his situations were never really his destination. He knew from God's track record in his life that for every trial and tragedy he experienced, there was a triumph. For every valley and vicissitude, there was a victory. So David declared that he would *bless the Lord at all times*. He would praise God even in his pain.

That should be great news for somebody today who's been dealing with disappointment and despair, and you can't seem to find your way out. It should help somebody who has been dealing with the real raw material of life – sickness in your body, loss of a loved one, relationship problems, difficulties on your job, more month than you have money.

And it should help somebody to see, like David, that your current situation is not your final destination... that trouble don't last always… that the God we serve might not come when we want God to come, but God is an on-time God. *So we can praise God today, even with what we are going through.*

And if David doesn't convince you with his testimony, there's a young teenage woman that I want to present to some, and introduce to others. In the Gospel of Luke there's a young teenage woman who can tell us a thing or two about praising God in and through our pain.

This young, teenage woman received news that would change her life, challenge her relationships, and cause some of those in her inner and outer circles to talk about her.

Luke tells us in the Gospel that this young teenage woman got some news that most teenagers never want to receive. The word tells us that the angel Gabriel stopped by to tell her that she was pregnant. But how could it be, as she was a virgin, and had not yet known her fiancé – as they had been abstinent?

And yet this young teenage woman got this news that she was pregnant, and not only that, but that her son, by *Immaculate Conception* would *be God's only begotten Son, the Savior of the whole world.*

But, in no small way, it really didn't matter who her son would be. Mary was a poor, young, single teenage mother-to-be. And some people in her community would do what some people in all communities would do when they heard about the circumstances of Mary's pregnancy. *They would talk about her, criticize her, ostracize her, castigate her, isolate her, shame her and shun her.*

But in the midst of the news that would bring her pain, Mary found it within herself to praise God. In her pain and uncertainty about her future, Mary sang a praise song – a magnificent song - to God (known as the Magnificat) –

"My soul magnifies the Lord,
and my spirit rejoices in God my Savior,
for he has looked on the humble estate of his servant.
For behold, from now on all generations will call me
blessed; for he who is mighty has done great things for
me, and holy is his name." *(Luke 1:46-49)*

I'm glad that Mary teaches us how to praise God in and through our pain. *We can and should praise God even in and through our pain.*

What's your praise song today? How might you sing in and through your pain, disappointment and despair? How might we do the same as David and as Mary? My song of praise today is -

"I do not know how long 'twill be –
or what the future hold for me,
but this I know, if Jesus leads me,
I'll get home some day!
(Charles Albert Tindley)

-40-
A PRAYER FOR THE MARYLAND STATE SENATE

(This prayer was delivered as the Invocation to open the Maryland State Senate session on Monday, March 29, 2017 in Annapolis, Maryland.)

O God, creator of all that is and is to be - from the rising of the sun, until the going down of the same – your name is worthy to be praised. God, we come together today to do what it is that you would will for us to do. We realize that you have created each of us with a unique calling and for a particular work. We come together hearing the cry that the ancient prophet intimated, a cry that is our collective prayer that you would live and breathe among us to "let justice roll down as waters, and righteousness as an ever-flowing stream." (Amos 5:24) O God we pray that you would see to it that as another ancient prophet intimated, we would "do justice, love kindness and walk humbly with you." (Micah 6:8)

Our prayer today is that you will align our hearts and minds with the cry of those who depend upon us the most - the needy, the left out, those who have the least among us. We pray for hearts of care, concern and compassion for the needy, and we pray for the wisdom to do what is right in your sight.

O God, we pray today for the great state of Maryland, and this country where we dwell. Bless those here and afar who lead us. Bless the places from which each of us has come. Bless every town and city, every community and home. Bless the schools where our children learn and the fields where they play.

Bless those who teach our children, those who protect our communities, and all of those who serve the common good. For we know that it is the common good that is your divine concern. Align our will with your will that we will see better, know better and do even better in the days that are ahead of us.

It is in your divine will that we seek to live today, that as yet another ancient prophet declared, we would know that you already know the plans you have for us, plans not to harm us, but plans for our well-being, and that your plans are to give us a future with hope. (Jeremiah 29:11)

And it is in that hope that we place our faith and trust today.

Amen.

-41-

ACROSS THE DIVIDES: DIMENSIONS OF DIFFERENCE AND IMPLICATIONS FOR THEOLOGIAL FIELD EDUCATORS IN THE 21ST CENTURY

(This essay was first delivered as the plenary lectures for the 34th Biennial Consultation of the Association for Theological Field Education, January 2017, St. Paul, Minnesota.)

SECTION ONE

Dimensions and Dynamics of Diversity in the 21st Century

In a world wrought with social, economic, political and religious upheaval – and with division endemic across much of society and much of the religious spectrum today, many people are asking the question, "Where is God?" Many students who come to theological schools today come asking the very same question, "Where is God?" Many students come today with more questions about the location of God in religion and society than they do with answers about who God is, and where God may be located.

And it is a part of the work of theological field educators to help students locate God so that they can then effectively lead people in the church and the world in the broader quest to locate God.

Over the past several years, in the United States and across the globe, we have become more divided along various lines. In the U.S., the social and political division that we now experience is not really new, but it challenges our sense of normalcy in ways that perhaps we have not been challenged in the past.

This division exists against the backdrop of a burgeoning diversity here and in other parts of the world. I had the opportunity to address a group of scholars in South Bend, Indiana two years ago where those in attendance were mostly North American, but interestingly the group included persons who were nearly equally Muslim, Jewish and Christian – and nearly equally white, black, Hispanic and Asian. I sense that this type of interreligious, intercultural engagement was not unique to that setting, but in some circles, is being challenged and brought into question in light of the overarching concern of what it means to be "American" today.

A part of this nation's sense of who it says it is is etched in one of our national credos – the Latin phrase *e-pluribus unum* – "Out of Many One." The implication here is that in the U.S, we have been, and continue to be, many. We are many cultures and ethnicities, many classes and social locations, many religions, many geographies, female and male, with many persuasions and ways of identifying what it means to be human. And yet, the vision that we say we share within the context of this "many" is a vision of somehow also becoming "one."

In any event, today we experience the challenge of living into this grand vision of realizing what it means to become *e pluribus unum.* Perhaps it is "Divides" which most clearly define us today, both in society and within religious communities. These Divides are seen in that we are Brown, White, Black, Asian and Indigenous, LBGTQI and 'straight", poor, working class, middle class and wealthy, Republican, Democrat and Independent, south and north, west and east, rural, suburban and urban, conservative, moderate and liberal, evangelical and progressive, non-denominational and mainline. These "Divides" are seen in that – politically and religiously - we are red, blue and indeed purple (yes purple).

Washington, DC – Anacostia and The Tale of Two Cities

I was born in Washington, DC in the 1960's. It was at a time when - I did not realize until I was a teenager – that the nation's capital was effectively a segregated the city. I grew up in a section of DC called Anacostia. For those of us who have grown up in the District of Columbia, lived there for any period of time, or visited and stayed for any length of time, we have come to realize that "Anacostia" in many ways is a euphemism for what it means to live east of the Anacostia River. This river effectively divides DC into east and west, and divides the city in more general ways along lines of what it means to grow up relatively poorer or richer – which is generally evident in the quality of schools, hospitals, policing/safety, roads, and so on. In many ways, to borrow a theme from Charles Dickens' great novel, this speaks to *the tale of two cities*.

Anecdotally, to have been reared in Anacostia carried with it a number of assumptions about who one might become, and the length and breadth of one's social mobility in life. To be from Anacostia effectively meant that one was reared in a socially segregated space where at the time of my upbringing was well over 85 percent Black, and largely populated by poor, working-class, and at-best barely above middle-class persons.

This is to say that growing up, to go anywhere west of the Anacostia River meant to cross over into another completely different socio-economic reality. This pronounced "Divide" in the nation's capital did not really dawn on me until I enrolled in Wesley Theological Seminary in my mid-20's. Wesley Seminary is located on the far northwest side of the city in one of the wealthiest neighborhoods in the nation (Ward 3), and taking the drive to seminary for three years from my home, which was by then just outside the city where I grew up in Anacostia, Southeast DC, I would drive across this "Divide" daily. I'd drive across the Anacostia River through drug-infested, "blue light" neighborhoods where many young men and women would feel blessed to live to adulthood, then past the national Capitol building, and the grand embassies which house international diplomats, and by exclusive private clubs, which growing up, I did not even realize existed, and finally I'd arrive each day at the seminary.

Baltimore - Sandtown and another Tale of Two Cities

The 2015 riots in Baltimore, Maryland serve as another vivid reminder of "Divides". The Sandtown community was the home of the late Freddie Gray who died while in police custody in Baltimore in April 2015. In the aftermath of Mr. Gray's death, Sandtown found itself in the national spotlight as the epicenter of the riots that erupted across much of Baltimore. I have served in ministry and taught in and near Sandtown for over 25 years.

Sandtown encompasses roughly one square mile of Baltimore, which covers over 80 square miles. It has a poverty rate of well over 60 percent, a high school dropout rate of well over 50 percent, an unemployment rate of over 25 percent, the second highest heroin addiction rate, and one of the highest HIV/AIDS infection rates, per capita, in the U.S. Of the 344 murders in Baltimore in 2015, over 300 were committed in the zip code (21217) where Sandtown is located, along with the two zip codes immediately adjacent to it. And yet, within one mile of Sandtown - within walking distance - one can walk in relative safety in several different directions through the relative wealth of the Baltimore Harbor district, the mid-town Business district and the Mt. Vernon/Mt. Royal Arts district.

During the Baltimore riots, we witnessed looting and destruction of several drug stores and food markets – destruction and burning of houses, cars and church property. We witnessed lashing out with violence against police officers. We saw the presence of the Maryland National Guard planted down in the city to maintain order on the streets. We saw and experienced what appeared to be hopelessness.

Interestingly, during and in the aftermath of the Baltimore riots, I was contacted by numerous students who had chosen over the preceding few years to do their intercultural immersion studies with me in Baltimore. During these Baltimore Urban Intercultural Immersions, which are a part of the Practice of Ministry and Mission program at Wesley Seminary, and are designed to help students integrate their classroom learning in the core theological disciplines, within the context of learning in a culture other than their own, these students had spent several days living in Baltimore - walking, studying, praying and ministering in the same Sandtown community where Freddie Gray had lived and died, and communities like it around Baltimore.

Many of the students who contacted me in the aftermath of the riots first of all expressed an appreciation that they had had the opportunity to be immersed in ministry and culture in Baltimore, and to see and interact with people in the very neighborhoods – like Sandtown – that they were now seeing on television. Their experiences in Baltimore, in no small way, served to "humanize" what they were seeing on television and in social media. While on these immersions – *as we prayed with our feet, exegeted communities,* entered into the stories of the unhoused, the hungry, the unemployed, and mothers who had lost children to violence on the streets, and encountered churches struggling to remain relevant in gentrifying urban communities - these experiences had served to add texture, depth and relevance to these students' theological education process.

Two students were so moved by what they experienced during a Baltimore Urban Intercultural Immersion experience in the winter of 2016 that they felt called to return to Baltimore this past summer to spend the entire summer fulfilling a part of their field education requirements serving in an inner city ministry that provides healthcare and counseling services to persons affected by HIV/AIDS and other health issues and to those who are addicted. They had essentially sensed a calling to, as articulated by Dr. Leah Gunning Francis in her book *Ferguson and Faith*, to pray with their feet. (Francis 2015,19f.)

"Table" as a Place of Meeting for Bridging Divides

Over the course of more than a decade, I have also had the privilege of leading groups of scholars from Wesley Theological Seminary in immersion courses that retrace many of the steps of the American Civil Rights movement in Alabama during the 1950's and 60's. These groups are typically comprised of 7-30 masters or doctoral level students, faculty and staff, and we travel for up to two weeks through Birmingham, Montgomery and Selma, Alabama.

On all of these immersion experiences, the groups of participants have been very diverse. We are women and men; Native Americans, Hispanics, Whites, Asians and Blacks. We are from various Christian denominations.

We begin each day with singing, praying and reading Scripture as was the practice in the tradition of the Civil Rights movement. John Lewis, now a U.S. Congressman from Georgia, and one who labored on the front lines of the Civil Rights movement, has intimated that "We never went out without singing and praying." And so before leaving each morning, we pray, read Scripture, and sing freedom songs like "Oh Freedom," "We Shall Overcome," "There is a Balm", and "Ain't Gonne Let Nobody Turn Me Around."

As we travel, reflect and listen together - struggling through many of the difficult paths and realities of those who lived the Civil Rights movement - we invariably sense among ourselves the real possibility that culturally inclusive community - *Beloved Community* - can be realized in our lifetime, and that bridges can indeed be built to help us cross and healthily engage those things that divide us.

Each time we journey, my memory harkens back to one of our trips several years ago, where Dr. Eileen Guenther, a professor at Wesley Seminary who was a part of that study group, offered that it was a spiritual sung by many choirs, "I'm Gonna Sit at the Welcome Table," that played in her head throughout our experience (see *The American Organist*, November 2008). Invariably, one of the most moving parts of our time in Alabama is our walk together across the Edmund Pettus Bridge in Selma, where on March 7, 1965 (known as "Bloody Sunday") over 600 persons of various races and religions were beaten and turned back by police in their efforts to cross the bridge and march from Selma to Montgomery to demand voting rights for all people.

At the conclusion of each of these Alabama intercultural immersions, I am invariably struck by how far we as a society have come, *and how many "Divides" we've crossed*, and yet how many "Divides" are yet to be crossed. There is a real sense of hope – and a real sense of the presence of God in our small, diverse groups - as together we choose to be the *Beloved Community* with one another. We realize that it would not have been possible 50 years ago for 7-30 people of faith from diverse backgrounds to travel in relative peace and safety throughout Alabama. For me, these are real signs of the stones of hope that, as Dr. Martin Luther King, Jr. spoke about in 1963, can be hewn out of the mountains of despair among us, real signs that "Divides" among us can and must continue to be crossed.

SECTION TWO

Theological Field Education amidst Difference and Change

Perhaps, it is a fundamental task of theological field educators to help students to discern very clearly who and what they have said "yes" to. And so, we might begin a conversation around the "who' and the "what" by considering a view of vocational formation and contextual education as means of integrating core theological disciplines (systematics, the study of scripture, history, and ethics) with the more practical disciplines like spiritual formation, leadership development, church management/administration, and leadership in the preaching and teaching ministries in churches and other contexts. Vocational formation and contextual education imply a dialogical process that connects and engages the student, the seminary and ministry settings resulting in developed/well-formed spiritual leaders who are equipped to serve churches and religious communities faithfully and effectively, and support these various ministry contexts in their ministries of transforming people, communities and the world.

A Theoretical Framework for Discussing "Divide"

An overarching concern in addressing the matter of "Divides" regards what it means for faith communities to be relevant today. The reality is that America and the world are rapidly changing. No longer can we simply view ourselves in terms of black and white, Protestant and Catholic. Lewis Brown Griggs and Lente-Louise Louw, editors of the series of works "*Valuing Diversity: New Tools for a New Reality*", suggest that differences in culture, ethnicity, gender, race, perspectives, personality, style, values and feelings need to be honored and encouraged, not merely tolerated. The real value of diversity is that it produces synergistic interactions across "Divides". It is this synergy that produces unpredictable consequences in terms of breakthrough and results. (Griggs and Louw 1995, 159)

To place the yearning for human connectedness into context, I believe that the African construct of Ubuntu is most helpful. Ubuntu simply means "the quality of being human." It manifests itself through various human acts, clearly visible in social, political, and economic situations, as well as among family and forms of community.

According to sociolinguist Buntu Mfentana, Ubuntu "runs through the veins of Africans." Lente-Louise Louw elaborates on it, and states that the quality of being human for Africans is embodied in the oft-repeated proverb, "A person is a person through other people." A quote from Archbishop Desmond Tutu emphasizes the criticality of Ubuntu, "You might have much of the world's riches, and might have a portion of authority, but if you have no Ubuntu, you do not amount to much."

Why is this important in the light of the practice of theology in the West? Research data shows that the United States continues to become more diverse or "different". Our difference at home is seen in that –

- Whites are the slowest growing segment of the U.S. population at .5%. Projections indicate that there will be a White minority (or no racial/ethnic majority) in the U.S. by 2044.
- There are at least 3.3 million Muslims in the U.S., and that number is likely to double by 2050 (Pew Research Center).
- There are at least 55.3 million Hispanics in the U.S. (17.4% of the population), with a projected 120 million Hispanics in the U.S. by 2060.
- Asians make up 5.8% of the U.S. population, and make up 36% of immigrants, overtaking Hispanics.

China is the fastest growing immigrant group in the U.S., passing Mexico.

- The 2nd fastest growing racial group in the U.S. is those claiming 2 or more races (bi-racial and multi-racial persons). This group has grown to at least 6.6 million people; 3.1% of the population.
- 41% of the world's migrants live in the West *(Christianity Today).*

(sources: U.S. Census Bureau, Pew Research Data, *Christianity Today*)

The Church and the Racial Divide

As it regards the church and the problem of race in America (as one form of "Divide"), in many ways, a pall remains over much – if not most - of the contemporary church and society. *Race continues to be the elephant in America's living room.* In their book, *Divided by Faith: Evangelical Religion and the Problem of Race,* Michael Emerson and Christian Smith developed a theory to explain why churches are racially exclusive enclaves despite Christian's ideals about being inclusive:

> Americans choose where and with whom to worship; race is one of the most important grounds on which they choose; so the more choices they have, the more their religious institutions will be segregated. (Emerson and Smith 2000, 154f.)

Through sociological analysis, Emerson and Smith tested that theory and found it to be valid. Churches are more segregated than schools, workplaces or neighborhoods. The least segregated sector of American society is also the least governed by choice; it's the military. Because white Protestants are the largest religious community in the U.S., they have the greatest choice as to with whom to gather. The authors point out that ninety-five percent of churches are effectively racially segregated, with 80 percent or more of their members being of the same race.

The result is that about 5 percent of religious congregations in the U.S. can fairly be considered multicultural/multiracial, with the majority of Christians engaging in what sociologists call homophily, or the desire to congregate with "birds of the same feather," with their congregations reflecting ethnoracial particularism. (Emerson and Smith)

The Church and Leadership

To remain faithful to their calling, churches and theological schools have more than a need; there is an obligation (a divine calling, a mandate) to examine our approaches to leadership development and vocational formation. Within the context of consistently rapid change, the church, like most other institutions today, is crying out for effective leadership. The church is in need of women and men who have a vision for a better future, and who possess the necessary skills to help move the church and society toward that future. Without transformational leadership, the church faces the prospects of losing its direction and failing to fulfill its mission.

The need for transformational leaders in the church is articulated by Dr. Lovett Weems in *Church Leadership*:

> "Leadership is needed for Christian communities as for other human communities, but not necessarily leadership in a fixed hierarchical model. Churches are likely to grow toward partnership among their members when there is a dynamic leadership behavior among a variety of people and not just one leader." (Weems 2012, 18)

Weems alludes to the leadership challenges confronting the contemporary church when he writes:

> "...the church has yet to explore the implications of leadership for the life of the church and for the role of its ordained leaders. The church desperately needs new wisdom that draws upon the richness of Christian teaching and tradition, and, at the same time, mines the best of contemporary research on leadership." (Weems)

Vocational Formation

As it pertains to vocational formation and the role of the seminaries and theological schools in participating in the task of developing church and religious leaders, leadership encompasses the skills, behaviors and attitudes in persons that are necessary to move Christian communities forward in the fulfillment of vital mission and ministry for the transformation of communities and the world.

In participating in the process of developing transformational leaders, theological field educators should give attention to future leaders being prayerful and discerning, discreet and strategic in determining what will be needed to lead churches and other ministry settings in moving people towards the specific vision - the preferred future - that God intends.

In essence, as theological field educators we play a critical role in helping future leaders see, articulate and realize *what it means to be pastoral-theologians – persons with the capacity and competence to think theologically and act pastorally as they live out their calling in ministry and service to the church and world.*

A Template for Discernment, Exploration and Formation

In preparing for ministry, ministry interns should be afforded opportunities to explore their vocational identity in four areas. The need for a clear sense of *imperative, imagination, innovation and integration* is necessary for engaging the daily, multiple, and frequently overwhelming demands of ministry within the context of congregations or other ministry settings today.

Imperative

Imperative points to God's intent and purpose – God's calling - for the minister's life within the context of service with and for the church and world. Arriving at the imperative of ministry involves a careful process of personal and communal discernment with the objective of arriving at clarity of calling. This speaks to the *divine and moral imperative – the calling* - that is placed upon persons seeking to engage in a life of Christian service.

Imagination

After careful discernment of *God's imperative and calling*, the ministry intern should then engage in processes of *imagination* as to the specific nature of their ministry and the form(s) that ministry might take for the particular individual and ministry context. With regard to imagination, Walter Brueggemann, in *The Prophetic Imagination* offers this perspective:

> I understand imagination is no doubt a complex epistemological process, to be the capacity to entertain images of meaning and reality that are beyond the givens of observable experience. That is, imagination is the hosting of the "otherwise"… beyond the evident. Without that we have nothing to say. We must take risks and act daringly to push beyond what is known to that which is hoped for and trusted, but not yet in hand. (Brueggemann 1978, 80f)

As a part of the imagining process, students in partnership with the ministry setting and theological school might engage in exploring questions such as, "What specific shape is my ministry taking?" "What am I beginning to envision, see and imagine as to God's preferred future for me in light of my gifts, graces and passions?" What risks am I willing to take to realize God's vision for my ministry, and for the church and world?"

Innovation

Innovation helps to draw upon the creative gifts that one has been given by God in the development of effective ministry. I refer to this as the "jazz" of ministry – the improvisational process which can result in significant ministry breakthroughs. *Innovation* speaks to the freedom and creative capacity that persons possess. It involves the capacity to see old things in new ways, to forge and create something viable from that which doesn't exist or has lost its vitality. It is the power to think and create on terms that reinforce personal sanctity, identity, and value of all persons, and ultimately to facilitate the creation of new shapes and forms of community and ministry.

Here, questions that might be explored are, "What innovative and creative approaches might be undertaken to build effective ministry and achieve desired outcomes? What gifts has God given the student and others (music, dance, poetry, drama, literature, liturgy, prayer, technology, capacity-building, consensus-building, etc.) that might make for creative and effective ministry?"

Integration

Finally, the process of *integration* can be seen as the capstone of the vocational formation process and involves the melding together of the various components of the educational experience – both in the classroom and in the ministry setting. Integration involves aspects of the *being, knowing and doing* of the student with the objective of forming ministry competencies that is seen in the development of highly effective religious leaders.

The principle of integration is related to the notion of synergy, and is the fruit of partnership and collegiality in the learning process, vocational formation and performance of ministry. The intent is to develop life-long patterns for leaders who are *well-developed, collegial and adaptive* within the contexts that they may be called to serve.

The Seminary Panel

I conclude by sharing an account of a recent panel conversation of seminary students. This experience sheds light on matters that might be given attention in thinking on the future of vocational discernment and the formation of future religious leaders.

The first observation about this seminary panel was the diversity of the group. Five of the six panelists were in their 20's or early 30's. They had arrived at seminary from six different places – Chicago, New York City, the Dominican Republic, Zimbabwe, Mississippi and Virginia – none had come from the city where they were now attending seminary. They were United Methodist (4), AME (1), and Baptist (1). They were Korean, Latino, African, White and African-American. Four were women.

This diversity reflects that of this particular seminary at-large, and points to the fact that theological education today looks quite different than it did forty years ago, and that perhaps this type of broadening diversity is reflective of where the church of today may be moving, and what will be required of its future leaders.

As these students reflected on their seminary experiences and how they thought their theological education would impact their future role as religious leaders, it was clear that each of these six persons articulated a vision of the church and a vision of their role as a religious leader that would move the church beyond traditional notions of what the church has been, and is to be, institutionally. And thus theirs were visions that shifted conceptions of Christian ministry, and the ways in which church leadership might be practiced in the future.

The collective insights/observations of these seminarians pointed to prospects of the 21st century church living into new and exciting forms of diversity, and prospects of churches of the future being shaped in ways that give impetus to several foundational concerns. Succinctly stated, these concerns are that:

1. The church must be led towards deeper, more intentional exploration and growth in the practice of *spiritual disciplines* as means towards deepening faith and creating community.
2. The church must engage in processes that encourage the ongoing development of competencies in the *art of leadership* that are sensitive to cultural inclusion

and the changes that are incumbent in new millennial reality.

3. The church must facilitate reflection/action relative to the burgeoning *globality* in our midst.
4. The church must facilitate an ongoing understanding and deeper engagement with *youth and young adult cultures (Millennials)*, which typically understand and appropriate the merging of cultures on levels that are more profound and pronounced than previous generations.
5. The church must facilitate constructive engagement and theological discourse across *cultures and theological/faith perspectives*.
6. The church must have the capacity to continue in organizing, developing and cultivating *strong partnerships and collaborations* (with students, local churches, judicatories, interfaith and non-religious entities).

Conclusion

In summary, the development of competencies in these and other areas among future leaders could serve to help leaders effectively engage in the ongoing work of transforming churches and faith communities of the future, and play critical roles in helping people to cross the many "Divides" that will continue to present themselves.

-42-

STONES OF HOPE (REVISITED)

(This message was delivered as the Commencement Address for the Graduate Theological Foundation, South Bend, Indiana on May 8, 2015.)

First, I would like to express my appreciation to Dr. Kendra Clayton, the Board of Directors of the Graduate Theological Foundation, the faculty, students and administration for the very kind invitation and opportunity to share with you on this momentous occasion. It is quite an honor to return to the Foundation, which has been one of my intellectual homes – an institution where I was a graduate student, and where I have been privileged to serve as a member of the faculty for over a decade.

And especially to the 2015 graduating class of the Graduate Theological Foundation, I offer words of congratulations and blessing to you, your families and the people you serve.

I am reminded of a portion of a simple poem by the great American poet Langston Hughes that encourages us to -

Hold fast to dreams
For when dreams go
Life is a barren field
Frozen with snow. ("Dreams")

It is my sense that one of the things that people of faith and conscience wrestle with the most, and seek to hold to - in any variety of traditions, perspectives, persuasions and systems of belief – including those of the Abrahamic faith traditions – Judaism, Islam and Christianity - is the matter of hope. The yearning to comprehend and appropriate hope is something that we all hold in common.

These are days of tremendous change and challenge in our world. From the collapse of domestic and global economics that affect all of us – to the wars that are now being fought in various places across the globe - to natural catastrophes – to the proliferation of violence that affects many people and communities across America and the world, these are days of unprecedented change and challenge.

And amidst this, there is yet this yearning for hope among us. German theologian Jürgen Moltmann wrote about hope in this way – "Hope alone is to be called "realistic" because it alone takes seriously the possibilities with which all reality is fraught. Hope does not take things as they happen to stand or to lie, but as progressing, moving things with possibilities of change." (Moltmann 1993, 25)

In one of his sermons, "The Meaning of Hope," Rev. Dr. Martin Luther King, Jr. defined hope as that quality which is "necessary for life". King asserted that hope was to be viewed as "animated and undergirded by faith and love." In his mind, if you had hope, you had faith in something. Thus, for King, hope shares the belief that "all reality hinges on moral foundations." Hope was, for him, the refusal to give up "despite overwhelming odds."

Indeed hope is not easily attained. In his book *Hope on a Tightrope*, philosopher Cornel West cautions against a false sense of security in hope, yet unborn. He points out that real hope is grounded in a particularly messy struggle and it can be betrayed by naive projections of a better future that ignore the necessity of doing real work. For West, real hope is closely connected to attributes like courage, faith, freedom and wisdom. It comes out of a context of struggle, and points to a future filled with the possibilities of promise and progress.

The hope that Moltmann, King and West wrote of is that which beckons us to love everybody – both our enemies and allies. This hope helps us to see that we can (and must) resist giving up on one another because our lives together are animated by the belief that we share in a common destiny. In his famous "I Have a Dream" speech delivered in our Nation's Capital in the summer of 1963, Dr. King shared that a part of his dream was that we would be able "to hew out of the mountain of despair, a stone of hope."

What hope does is it moves us closer toward Dr. King's notion of *Beloved Community*. Hope beckons us to dream of a better world. Hope for a better world is ultimately rooted and grounded in our shared sense that there is real potential for each of us to change the world. This is what Mohandas Gandhi meant when he encouraged those of his day to "be the change that you want to see in the world."

Every few years, I have the privilege of leading a group of scholars from Wesley Theological Seminary in a doctoral immersion course that retraces many of the steps of the American Civil Rights movement in Alabama. I journeyed with one group this past winter, and will journey with another group of students this August.

The group in January was typical of others with which I have worked over the years. We reflected much of the diversity of society today. We were Hispanic, Native American and Asian, white and black, female and male, and from multiple Christian faith traditions. As we traveled in January, we prayed, sang, and shared our thoughts together. We cried together on occasion, and we rejoiced together.

As we traveled, my memory harkened back to one of our trips several years ago, where Dr. Eileen Guenther, a professor at Wesley Seminary who was a part of that study group, offered that it was a spiritual sung by many choirs, "I'm Gonna Sit at the Welcome Table," that played in her head throughout our experience (see *The American Organist*, November 2008). Dr. Guenther said that she thought about the variety of tables that we encountered as we traveled through Alabama (which at a time had come to be known as the cradle of the confederacy and as a bastion of racial segregation in America):

- Lunch counters of restaurants where all had not been welcome (in the past);
- The dining room table in the parsonage of Dexter Avenue Baptist Church, in Montgomery, where we were told, the Southern Christian Leadership Conference was formed;
- The kitchen table of the same parsonage where Dr. King searched his soul and felt God telling him to press on with his work;

- The tables at which the people at Sixteenth Street Baptist Church served us lunch, tables placed adjacent to the site of the tragic bombing on September 15, 1963 that killed four young girls;
- The tables around which members of our group gathered to share stories as victims of discrimination, of their courageous work in the Civil Rights movement (and other freedom and human rights movements), and their lament over a lack of awareness of what was going on at that time in America's history.

At the conclusion of each of our doctoral immersions in Alabama, I am invariably struck by how far we as a society have come - and yet how far we have to go. There is a real sense of hope – and the presence of God in our small, diverse groups - as together we choose to be the *Beloved Community* with one another. We realize that it would not have been possible 40 years prior for 7-30 people of such diverse backgrounds to travel in relative peace and safety throughout Alabama. For me, these are real signs of the stones of hope that can be hewn out of the mountains of despair among us.

And so wherever we find ourselves in the world, and however we seek to find hope in the living of these days, we are beckoned to heed, again the poetic words of Langston Hughes –

Hold fast to dreams

For if dreams die

Life is a broken-winged bird

That cannot fly. (“Dreams”)

-43-

Closing Prayer - A Christmas Prayer (2016)

O God, as you wrapped yourself in flesh over 2000 years ago and sent your Son into the world, we come to another Christmas celebrating the gift that is Christ.

We are grateful for your abiding presence in the world over the ages, and appreciate the ways you are present with us today, and thus we are grateful for how you will be present with us in the days ahead.

As Jesus was born poor, to an unwed parent, and on the margins of his world - we pray during this Christmas season especially for those who likewise exist on the margins of our world - the hungry, the homeless and those without adequate healthcare.

We pray for all of those who exist in the abyss of apparent hopelessness, lovelessness, and meaninglessness.

Bless O God, this nation and the world. Bless those who lead now and will lead in the days ahead - in elected and appointive office. Bless them with a portion of your wisdom, justice and compassion.

Most importantly, help us all to see your face as evidenced in Christ in all that we seek to be and do, and wherever we find ourselves.

May your grace and mercy abide in our lives during this Christmas season and forevermore. Amen.

References and Bibliography

Alexander, Michelle (2012). *The New Jim Crow: Mass Incarceration in the Age of Colorblindness.* New York: The New Press.

Baker-Fletcher, Garth (1993). *Somebodyness: Martin Luther King, Jr. and the Theory of Dignity.* Minneapolis, MN: Fortress Press.

Baldwin, Lewis V. (1991). *There is a Balm in Gilead: The Cultural Roots of Martin Luther King, Jr.* Minneapolis: Fortress Press.

Baldwin, Lewis V. (1993). *To Make the Wounded Whole: The Cultural Legacy of Martin Luther King, Jr.* Minneapolis: Fortress Press.

Bonhoeffer, Dietrich (1963). *The Cost of Discipleship.* New York: Macmillan Publishing Company.

Brueggemann, Walter (1978). *The Prophetic Imagination.* Minneapolis, MN: Fortress Press.

Coates, Ta-nisi (2015). *Between the World and Me.* New York: Penguin/Random House.

Cone, James (1986). *A Black Theology of Liberation.* Maryknoll, NY: Orbis Books.

Davis, Angela (2016). *Freedom is a Constant Struggle: Ferguson, Palestine, and the Foundations of a Movement.* Chicago: Haymarket Books.

Dear, John (1988). "The Experiments of Gandhi: Nonviolence in the Nuclear Age" in *Fellowship.* New York: Fellowship of Reconciliation, January/February.

Doulgas, Kelly Brown (2015). *Stand Your Ground: Black Bodies and the Justice of God.* Maryknoll, NY: Orbis Books.

DuBois, W.E.B.(1903). *The Souls of Black Folk.* Chicago: A.G. McClurg and Co.

Dyson, Michael Eric (2008). *April 4, 1968 – Martin Luther King, Jr.'s Death and How it Changed America.* New York: Basic Books.

Dyson, Michael Eric (2009). *Can You Hear Me Now?* New York: Basic Books.

Dyson, Michael Eric (2017). *Tears We Cannot Stop: A Sermon to White America.* New York: McMillan.

Dyson, Michael Eric (2016). *The Black Presidency: Barack Obama and the Politics of Race in America.* New York: Houghton Muffin Harcourt Publishing

Emerson, Michael and Christian Smith (2000). *Divided by Faith: Evangelical Religion and the Problem of Race.* Oxford, UK: Oxford University Press.

Fisher, Mary Pat and Lee W. Bailey (2000). *An Anthology of Living Religions.* Upper Saddle River, NJ: Prentice Hall.

Fluker, Walter E. Fluker and Catherine Tumber, eds. (1998). *A Strange Freedom: The Best of Howard Thurman.* Boston Beacon Books.

Francis, Gunning Francis (2015). *Ferguson and Faith: Sparking Leadership and Awakening Community.* St. Louis: Chalice Press.

Frankl, Victor (1959). *Man's Search for Meaning.* Boston, MS: Beacon Press.

Franklin, Robert M. (1990). *Liberating Visions: Human Fulfillment and Social Justice in African American Thought.* Minneapolis: Fortress Press.

Gandhi, Mohandas K. (1942). *Non-violence in Peace and War,* Vol. 1. Ahmedabad: Navajivan Publishing House.

Gandhi, Rajmohan. (April 27, 1995). "Gandhi's Unfulfilled Legacy: Prospects for Reconciliation in Racial/Ethnic Conflict" (1995 Cynthia Wedel Lecture). Washington, DC: Church's Center for Theology and Public Policy, Wesley Theological Seminary.

Griggs, Lewis Brown and Lente-Louise Louw (1995). *Valuing Diversity: New Tools of a New Reality,* New York: McGraw Hill.

Heschel, Abraham Joshua (1951). *Man is Not Alone: A Philosophy of Religion.* New York: Farrar, Straus and Giroux.

Hunt, C. Anthony (2005). *Blessed are the Peacemakers: A Theological Analysis of the Thought of Howard Thurman and Martin Luther King, Jr.* Lima, OH: Wyndham Hall Press.

Hunt, C. Anthony (2006). *And Yet the Melody Lingers: Essays, Sermons and Prayers on Religion and Race.* Lima, OH: Wyndham Hall Press.

Hunt, C. Anthony (2011). *My Hope is Built: Essays, Sermons and Prayers on Religion and Race, vol. 2.* Lima, OH: Wyndham Hall Press.

Hunt, C. Anthony (2016). *Keep Looking Up: Sermons on the Psalms.* Lima, OH: Wyndham Hall Press.

Hunt, C. Anthony (2001). *Upon the Rock: A Model for Ministry with Black Families.* Lima, OH: Wyndham Hall Press.

Hunt, C. Anthony (2004). "Martin Luther King, Jr.: Resistance, Nonviolence and Community" in *Black Leaders and Ideologies in the South: Resistance and Nonviolence*, Preston King and Walter Earl Fluker, eds. London, UK: Critical Review of Social and Political Philosophy.

King, Martin Luther, Jr. (1986). "Pilgrimage to Nonviolence," in *A Testament of Hope: The Essential*

Writings and Speeches of Martin Luther King, Jr. James Melvin Washington, ed. New York: Harper Collins.

King, Martin Luther, Jr. (1963). *Strength to Love.* New York: Harper.

King, Martin Luther Jr. (1958). *Stride Toward Freedom: The Montgomery Story.* Boston: Beacon Press.

King, Martin Luther, Jr. (1968). *Where Do We Go from Here: Chaos or Community?* Boston: Beacon Press.

Kushner, Harold (1981). *When Bad Things Happen to Good People.* New York: Schocken Books.

Loder, Ted (2000). *My Heart in My Mouth: Prayers for our Lives*. Philadelphia, PA: Innisfree Press.

Marsh, Charles. (2005). *The Beloved Community: How Faith Shapes Social Justice from the Civil Rights Movement.* New York: Basic Books.

Marty, Martin (1984). *Pilgrims in their Own Land.* New York: Penguin Books.

McMickle, Marvin (2006). *Where Have All the Prophets Gone?* Cleveland, OH: Pilgrim Press.

Merton, Thomas (1964). *Gandhi on Nonviolence.* New York: New Directions.

Moltmann, Jürgen (1993). *A Theology of Hope.* Minneapolis, MN: Fortress.

Myrdal, Gunnar (1944). *An American Dilemma: The Negro Problem and Modern Democracy.* New York: Harper and Row.

Oates, Stephen B. (1982). *Let the Trumpet Sound: The Life of Martin Luther King, Jr.* New York: Harper and Row.

Obama, Barack (2006). *The Audacity of Hope: Thoughts on Reclaiming the American Dream.* New York: Three Rivers Press.

Peterson, Eugene H. (2003). *The Message – Remix – The Bible in Contemporary Language.* Colorado Springs, CO: Navpress.

Pollard, Alton B. Pollard, III. (1992). *Mysticism and Social Change: The Social Witness of Howard Thurman.* New York: Lang.

Rauschenbusch, Walter (1945). *A Theology of the Social Gospel.* Louisville, KY: Westminster John Knox Press.

Roberts, J. Deotis (2000). "Gandhi and King: On Conflict Resolution," in *Shalom Papers: A Journal of Theology and Public Policy,* ed. Victoria J. Barnett. Washington, DC: Church's Center for Theology and Public Policy, Vol. 11, No. 2, Spring 2000.

Shannon, William H. Shannon (1996). *Seeds of Peace: Contemplation and Nonviolence.* New York: Crossroad Publishing. *Songs of Zion* (1974). Nashville: Abingdon Press.

Smith, Huston (1991). *The World's Religions.* New York: Harper Collins.

Smith, Kenneth and Ira Zepp, Jr. (1974). *Search for the Beloved Community.* Valley Forge, PA: Judson Press.

Stevenson, Bryan (2014). *Just Mercy: A Story of Justice and Redemption.* New York: Penguin Random House.

Thurman, Howard (1976). *Jesus and the Disinherited.* Boston: Beacon Press.

Thurman, Howard (1973). *The Mood of Christmas.* Richmond, IN: Friends United Press.

Thurman, Howard (1971). *The Search of Common Ground.* Richmond, IN: Friends United Press.

Tillich, Paul (1952). *The Courage to Be.* New Haven, CT: Yale University Press.

Wallis, Jim (2017). *America's Original Sin: Racism, White Privilege and the Bridge to a New America.* Grand Rapids, MI: Brazos Press.

Wallis, Jim (2013). *On God's Side; What Religion Forgets and Politics Hasn't Learned about Serving the Common Good.* Grand Rapids, MI: Brazos Press.

Washington, James Melvin, ed. (1986). *A Testament of Hope: The Essential Writings and Speeches of Martin Luther King, Jr.* New York: Harper Collins.

Watley, William D. (1985). *Roots of Resistance: The Nonviolent Ethic of Martin Luther King, Jr.* Valley Forge, PA: Judson Press.

Weems, Lovett H., Jr. (2010). *Church Leadership: Vision, Team, Culture and Integrity.* Nashville, Abingdon Press.

West, Cornel (2008). *Hope on a Tightrope.* New York: Smiley Books.

West, Cornel (1993). *Race Matters.* Boston: Beacon Press.

Yates, Elizabeth (1964). *Howard Thurman: Portrait of a Practical Dreamer.* New York: John Day.

ABOUT THE AUTHOR

C. ANTHONY HUNT

A native of Washington D.C., Rev. Dr. C. Anthony Hunt currently serves as the Senior Pastor of Epworth Chapel United Methodist Church in Baltimore, MD, and as Professor of Systematic, Moral and Practical Theology and Permanent Dunning Distinguished Lecturer at the Ecumenical Institute of Theology, St. Mary's Seminary and University in Baltimore. He also teaches at Wesley Theological Seminary in Washington, DC, United Theological Seminary in Dayton, OH and at the Graduate Theological Foundation in Mishawaka, IN, where he is a faculty Fellow and E. Franklin Frazier Professor of African-American Studies.

He is a graduate of the University of Maryland, and holds advanced degrees from Troy State University, Wesley Theological Seminary and the Graduate Theological Foundation. Additionally, he has completed post-graduate studies at St. Mary's Seminary and University, Baltimore, MD; the Center of Theological Inquiry, Princeton NJ; the University of Oxford, UK, and the Institute of Certified Professional Managers, James Madison University, Harrisonburg, Va.

Anthony is the author of seven other books including, *Keep Looking Up: Sermons on the Psalms* (2016), *My Hope is Built: Essays, Sermons and Prayers on Religion and Race, vol. 2* (2011), *And Yet the Melody Linger: Essays, Sermons and Prayers on Religion and Race* (2006), and

Blessed are the Peacemakers: A Theological Analysis of the Thought of Howard Thurman and Martin Luther King, Jr. (2005), and over 100 articles and chapters on matters pertaining to religion and society. He is also an active blogger at www.newurbanminstry.blogspot.com.